MW01133701

With much appreciation to Paola Antonelli,
Senior Curator in the Department of Architecture and Design
at MoMA, who, along with Christian Larsen,
Curatorial Assistant, believed that these *Esquire* covers
of the 1960s should take their place in the
permanent collections of the Museum of Modern Art.

601 West 26th Street, 18th Floor
New York, NY 10001, USA
www.assouline.com
Tel.: 212 989-6810 Fax: 212 647-0005

ISBN: 978 2 7594 0434 6

Writer and Designer: George Lois
Digital Design and Composition: Luke Lois, Good Karma Creative
Color Separation: Luc Alexis Chasleries, Luc A.C. Retouching

Printed in China

GEORGE LOIS

THE ESQUIRE COVERS @ MoMA

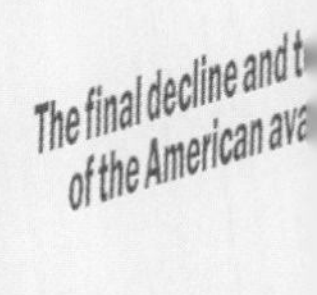

To celebrate the installation of the
George Lois Esquire covers
in the permanent collection of
The Museum of Modern Art,
you are cordially invited to a reception and
exhibit of 32 of his iconic covers.

MoMA
11 West 53rd Street
(Please use entrance to
The Ronald S. and Jo Carole Lauder Building)
Wednesday, April 30
8:00 to 10:00 pm
Architecture & Design Galleries
Third Floor

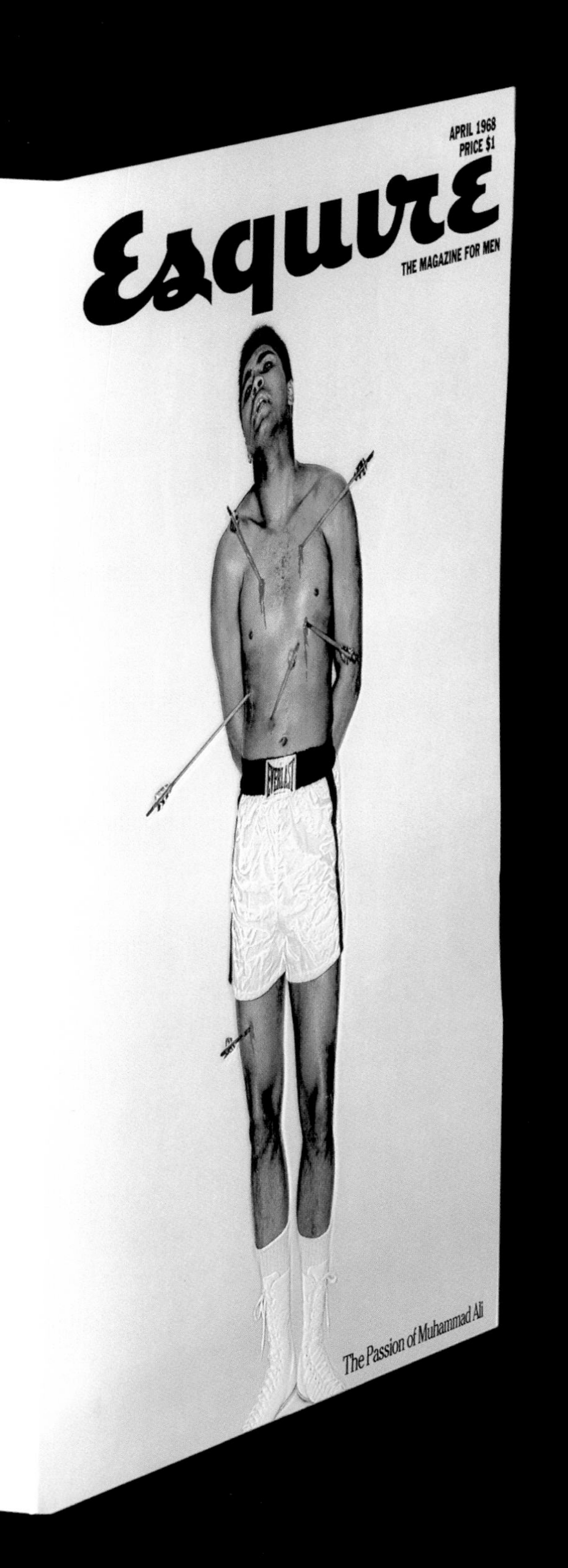

*AN INVITATION TO A RECEPTION
FOR THE INSTALLATION AND YEARLONG EXHIBIT
OF THE GEORGE LOIS* ESQUIRE *COVERS
AT THE MUSEUM OF MODERN ART, APRIL 30, 2008.*

GEORGE LOIS BEING INTERVIEWED AT PAPERT KOENIG LOIS IN 1964.

Nuclear Bomb
testing

GEORGE LOIS SPARKED THE CREATIVE REVOLUTION IN THE ADVERTISING WORLD IN THE 1960s (SHOWN HERE DIRECTING JOE NAMATH IN A TELEVISION COMMERCIAL, 1972). LOIS CREATED THE ESQUIRE *COVERS IN HIS SPARE TIME.*

HAROLD T.P. HAYES, A WHITE SOUTHERN LIBERAL, AN EX-MARINE CAPTAIN, A TROMBONE PLAYER, AND THE GREATEST MAGAZINE EDITOR IN AMERICAN HISTORY, GOING APE ONE DAY IN THE OFFICES OF ESQUIRE *MAGAZINE.*

GEORGE LOIS,
PERHAPS RECEIVING INSPIRATION
FOR AN ESQUIRE *COVER*
(SEE PAGE 160).

CONTENTS

GEORGE LOIS: THE ESQUIRE COVERS

From 1962 to 1972, George Lois created some of the most arresting and iconic images in the history of the magazine cover. With his uniquely uncompromising point of view, Lois exploited the communicative power of the mass-circulated front page to stimulate minds and provoke public debate. The sensational effect these covers had on the public was an obvious advantage for *Esquire*'s circulation, but their lasting importance was that they forced Americans to confront controversial issues such as racism, feminism, religion, and the Vietnam War. These images hit the public like a punch in the face, their messages artfully communicated with force and immediacy.

In 2008, the Museum of Modern Art, in New York, opened a yearlong exhibition dedicated to Lois, featuring 32 of his covers alongside original artwork, photographs, contact sheets, and other ephemera as a means of explaining the creative process behind these deceptively simple yet complex designs. With the wholehearted support of *Esquire* editor Harold Hayes and the collaboration of photographers Carl Fischer, Timothy Galfas, Art Kane, Harold Krieger, Ira Mazer, Dick Richards, and Tasso Vendikos, the full extent of Lois' design talent shines as he translates daring ideas into visually stunning, eloquent images. As paradigms of graphic and communication design, the covers are significant additions to MoMA's collection.

Viewed as a collection now, nearly fifty years since they first appeared on the newsstands, the covers serve as a visual time line and a window onto the turbulent events of the 1960s. Initially received as jarring and prescient statements, Lois' *Esquire* covers have since become essential to the iconography of American culture.

CHRISTIAN LARSEN

CHRISTIAN LARSEN

Curatorial Assistant, Research and Collections
Department of Architecture and Design
The Museum of Modern Art

GEORGE LOIS DRAWING THE ROUGH LAYOUT OF HIS 1969 ESQUIRE *COVER OF ANDY WARHOL DROWNING IN HIS OWN SOUP.*

GEORGE LOIS' ATELIER
AT HIS AD AGENCY
PAPERT KOENIG LOIS, 1965.

GEORGE LOIS ON THE TERRACE OF HIS AD AGENCY LOIS HOLLAND CALLAWAY, OVERLOOKING CENTRAL PARK, 1969.

EDITOR HAROLD HAYES BELTING IT OUT IN HIS ESQUIRE *MAGAZINE CORNER OFFICE ON MADISON AVENUE, 1962.*

IT NEVER OCCURRED BEFORE.
IT HAS NEVER HAPPENED SINCE.

Here is a full decade, arguably America's most roisterous and chaotic, nailed and impaled on the monthly disruptive covers of *Esquire* magazine. How staggering to think that in the same time period dissected by these covers *four hundred and seventy-five thousand other covers*, on other magazines, were published by the millions and sank without a ripple. But George Lois' *Esquire* covers are immutable. They encapsulate each tumult and retrieve it at a glance. Some are scorched into our memory... like the boyish Lieutenant Calley, appallingly casual amid the ghosts of the irresistible Vietnamese toddlers he ordered machine-gunned. Others delight us anew...like the shameless Nixon, being made up to the eyeballs, lusting after the office he would predictably besmirch.

The story of how these covers came to be is as riveting as the works themselves. They are the sole creation of one man, yet somehow the product of two: George Lois and his great pal, editor Harold Hayes. Both talented and urbane, both acutely, even painfully, sensitive to the seismic changes unfolding around them. Hayes was obsessed with editing and navigating his magazine until it became a publication like no other, standing alone as the reflective and articulate conscience of a time gone awry.

But it wasn't until Hayes importuned Lois to reinvent the magazine cover, imprinting it as personally and irrevocably as he had revolutionized the world of advertising, that we readers understood and hopped on board. Intuitively, George grasped the essence of each issue, transforming it into a jarring image that instantly informed and disturbed. Month after month, new covers leapt from the newsstands, grabbing our eyes and dunking our minds into yet another hairpin turn of those roller-coaster '60s. So turn these pages and turn back the years, with these haunting, taunting monthly works of art. And be grateful that you aren't rationed to viewing them one at a time, with an endless four weeks' wait before each new one, as my generation was, awaiting with joy the next graphic miracle that George Lois would spring on us.

RON HOLLAND, 1967

RON HOLLAND

This article, reprinted from Adweek, *October 5, 1981, shows Hayes at his editorial best–taking flak and deflating specious criticism.*

HAROLD HAYES ON GEORGE LOIS AND THOSE ESQUIRE COVERS

HAROLD HAYES, 1962

I remember walking George Lois' Sonny Liston cover around to all the department heads; to the advertising director, the advertising promotion manager, the circulation director, the circulation manager, the publisher, the president, and, finally to the chairman of the board. Since it was intended for the December issue, everyone understood that I understood it was to be Christmasy. No one at *Esquire* would ever try to tell the editor what to do, but it would have been unthinkable for anyone,from the chairman to the cleaning lady, to expect the December issue, which traditionally marked the season with its heaviest yield of ad pages–twice that of an ordinary issue–*not* to be Christmasy. It goes without saying, I had said earlier to George Lois to make sure he didn't forget that the December issue had to be Christmasy. Since the magazine back then was put together three months in advance of its appearance, and since the December issue, in order to realize its maximum selling force, was moved back an extra week or so to come out before Thanksgiving, the climate–in keeping with the true calendar–was hot and sticky, as I recall, decidedly unfestive. Of these several gentlemen with whom I was obliged to discuss the proposed cover, the most direct was the circulation manager, a veteran hawker who in Yuletides past had favored encasing the issue in a gold-tinsel box.

"Jesus Christ, Hayes," he said now, "you call *that* Christmasy? What the hell are you trying to *do* to us?"

I have never known a talent quite as pure as that of George Lois. It is impossible to control or regulate, and I suspect that if anyone or anything ever succeeded completely in doing so, it would simply disappear. That George is himself one of his own most enthusiastic admirers doesn't have anything to do with it; he is every bit as good as he thinks he is. In the ten years we worked together (he in his office usually, I in mine), we collaborated only to the extent that I took pains to be sure he knew what we would be doing inside the issue. After that, his imagination could be trusted to do its work alone.

With his very first cover for *Esquire*, in October 1962, the 31-year-old Lois had earned that unusual freedom. Robert Benton was the art director in those days, and it is no disservice to Benton, now a successful film director and writer, to disclose that neither he nor I had the slightest idea of how to make a cover work. Both of us were young and inexperienced, with enough authority to produce the magazine but not enough of whatever it took to persuade anyone else, ourselves included, we knew how to produce effective covers. So, in desperation, we tried producing three for an issue, then five, and finally, near wit's end, ten, hoping somehow through diversity to smother our ineptitude. The consequence of such extremes, of course, was the resolution of choice by committee vote, and inevitably, as any dummy could have told us, the least effective of the ten was chosen.

Lois changed all that. I called the art director who was getting so much attention in the advertising press, so I could get his advice on how to create better covers. We talked about our next issue and he agreed to create the cover. Then he did it. A week later, a messenger brought it over, a full-size color print of a defeated athlete in an empty arena tying neatly into a Lois sports prediction featured inside. The photograph had been assigned, directed by Lois on location, frame-matted, and covered with glistening acetate. All the type was in place, the logo, the cover line (which George had written), and the cover date. It was superb!

Even the department heads could see this was work better than anything Benton or I could do, and from that time on, George Lois, 12 blocks away in his advertising office, conceived and produced some 92 covers for *Esquire* magazine. Getting back to the Liston cover…

"Well, what the hell," I said to the circulation guy and his stunned colleagues down the hall, "It *is* Christmasy. Look at the Santa Claus hat."

Nobody thought that was very funny, or that there was any wit to be granted in the magazine's mockery of its own commercial intent.

Strong as it remains even now, you need to do some remembering to appreciate how strong it was back then. Sonny Liston was a "bad" black

who beat up "good" blacks, like Floyd Patterson; there was no telling what he might do
to a white man. In 1963, when this was the sort of possibility that preyed
on white men's minds everywhere, George Lois' Christmasy cover was something
more than an inducement for readers to buy Dad extra shaving soap.
In the national climate of 1963, thick with racial fear, Lois' angry icon insisted on
several things: The split in our culture was showing; the notion of racial
equality was a bad joke; the felicitations of this season—goodwill to all men, etc.—
carried irony more than sentiment. What it was, the intervening years
now make clear, was the perfect magazine cover—a single, textless image that measured
our lives and the time we lived them in quite precisely to the moment.
From one of the survivors of those times, the claim now comes that the
Liston cover cost *Esquire* $750,000 in canceled advertising.
That's some price to pay for having tried to say something on a magazine cover...
and magazines, as everyone knows who works with them,
are in business to make money, not lose it. There are, of course, all sorts of grand
and lofty ideals by which one may justify principle over profit.
Nevertheless, under circumstances I have come better to understand over the years,
the proprietors of *Esquire* were pretty forbearing about the Liston cover fallout
inasmuch as I did keep my job, and George Lois did continue designing our covers.
The real question that arises from all this, with implications
as appropriate to the Falwellian Age as the Listonian, is: Did *Esquire* management
make the right business decision? Here, hindsight may be more helpful than
a two-year symposium at Harvard Business School.
Lois stayed (and, if anything, grew more troublesome to handle)
but the business prospered! It is therefore reasonable to suggest that the
growing number of advertisers who found that particular magazine
in those years congenial to their commercial interests might not have if George Lois
had not been designing its covers. Try as I might, I am unable to conceive
of the *Esquire* of the '60s without George Lois.
I suspect the same is true for others who remember it today. One might even go so far
as to conclude, then, that with the loss of this inimitable element,
Esquire could have ceased to be *Esquire*. And if there should have been no *Esquire*,
how could anything have been made or lost from it? ■

GEORGE LOIS, SPEAKING TO EDITOR HAROLD HAYES:

“HAROLD, A MESSENGER IS ON HIS WAY TO YOU WITH YOUR COVER. BUT I GOTTA TELL YOU, PAL, THIS ONE IS REALLY GONNA CAUSE A LOT OF TROUBLE.”

HAROLD HAYES: “YEAH-H-H-H!”

Esquire
The Svetlana Papers
or: the advantage of being Stalin's daughter.

A talk celebrating Lois' collaboration with Harold Hayes (1926–1989), delivered at the Society of Publication Designers annual dinner in 2004, when Lois was presented with the Herb Lubalin Lifetime Achievement Award for editorial design, the only ever given to an adman.

GEORGE LOIS ON HAROLD HAYES AND THOSE ESQUIRE COVERS

GEORGE LOIS, 1964

In 1962, my ad agency was spearheading the change in advertising known as "The Creative Revolution!" That's when *Esquire*'s editor first approached me for advice on how to create a great cover.
When I met him for lunch at The Four Seasons, he was stylishly decked out in a white suit and waggling a skinny stogie, in keeping with his getup, Southern drawl, and poker-playing eyes. I told him that every "package design" should be at least as good as the product inside–and his *Esquire* was the best magazine product I ever read.
"You don't get great stuff from Baldwin and Capote and Talese and Wolfe with a management committee stumbling over each other, voting for the safest syntax." Harold understood, and that was the beginning of a beautiful friendship.
I instinctively understood that a trombone-playing Southern liberal who was also a marine reserve officer was one rare bird.
During the turbulent '60s, starting in 1962, I produced 92 covers for *Esquire*.
Every time a new visual editorial was delivered to Harold from my drawing table, *Esquire*'s publishers, editors, ad directors, and assorted bureaucrats crossed their hearts and fingers. I had always telegraphed the cover idea to Harold, usually over the phone–while it was Harold who often suggested the cover subject.
We spoke in shorthand and communicated with economy:
For Christmas, Hayes pleaded, fingering his pencil stogie,
"Ol' buddy, ya gotta compromise *this* time. Y'all gotta give me a goddamn *Christmas* cover!"
This led to America's first black Santa: Sonny Liston, the meanest man in the world.
Respirators were rushed to *Esquire*'s ad offices.
"Do a job on Svetlana," he asked.
"Oh, no," I moaned. "Not *another* magazine cover with her fink mug!"
Thus it came to pass that I painted her father's mustache on Svetlana Stalin:
The family resemblance was awesome.
For an issue that featured John Sack's account of an infantry company from basic training to 'Nam, I lifted a cry of pain from a young G.I.–
"*Oh my God–we hit a little girl.*"–and set it starkly in white against black.
When I asked Harold if he thought we would piss off America, he said,
"If they don't like what's on the cover, they can always buy *Vogue*, sweetheart."
That was 1966, a premature time for indicting that evil war.

For an issue on the decline of the American avant garde, we showed Andy Warhol drowning, literally, in his own soup. And Harold knew he'd find himself in deep water when I showed Muhammad Ali as the martyr Saint Sebastian for refusing to fight in a bad war. Harold lined up his fine Carolinian nose against my Bronx schnoz and put his Dixie neck on the chopping block once again. When a critical piece was being prepared on Humphrey for parroting his boss, I sat a Hubert dummy on ventriloquist LBJ's knee. It was a needed jab at Humphrey's failure to speak out against Vietnam. When the article wound up being laudatory, Hayes added a compromising "But in fairness to our Vice President, see page 106," because he couldn't bear to lose the cover. When I slapped a theater marquee on St. Paddy's Cathedral to illustrate an article on "The New Movies: Faith of our Children," Harold made the sign of the cross and took the heat. But the cover that truly tested the mettle of *Esquire*'s staff (and, indeed, the mettle of America itself) was a portrait of Lieutenant Calley, in the flesh. There he was, awaiting trial for his role in the My Lai massacre, posing with an obscene grin, surrounded by Vietnamese kids.
After receiving the obviously controversial cover, Harold called—as he always did after the smoke cleared. With a deep sigh, he gave me the verdict:
"Most detest it, George. But the smart ones love it."
"You going to chicken out?" I asked. "Nope," he said.
"That cover is what *Esquire* is all about." After one of his college-campus lectures, Harold called me from Arizona about the notorious Calley cover:
"The kids are having fistfights over this one, Lois. It's great!" When Roy Cohn wrote a self-serving piece on his gofer years with Joe McCarthy, I shot him with a tinsel halo, visibly pinned to his noggin by photographer Carl Fischer. Oblivious to its slashing irony, Cohn posed obligingly. The next day Harold called me, "Oh, you really nailed that sonofabitch." Always pressured by an unappreciative ad-sales staff, Harold half-heartedly pleaded, "They're clamoring for another girlie cover." I complied by showing a naked dame, squashed in a garbage can, headlined "The New American Woman: through at 21."

"Well, pal," was Harold's reaction, "you sure didn't disappoint me."
And then there was Nixon. When he ran for president in 1968,
we showed him being made up like a movie star.
"Nixon's last chance," went the caption. "(This time he'd better look right!)"
Promptly, Harold got an indignant call from Ron Ziegler, Nixon's mouthpiece,
complaining that *Esquire* was trying to depict his boss as a homosexual.
When I perpetrated a sham sighting of the elusive Howard Hughes,
the media crowd fell for it, not realizing it was a put-on.
Esquire's ad department went apoplectic. Harold merely chortled.
Obviously, *Esquire*'s brass put up with my shenanigans because
during those Hayes years circulation went from 500,000 to almost 2,000,000
(dumping right back down to 500,000 when Hayes and I bailed out).
The *Esquire* covers were uncensored commentaries on serious issues in our own style.
Under the benign and courtly aegis of publisher Arnold Gingrich,
Harold gave me greater latitude than anyone before or since thought possible
from a mass periodical. "Pictorial Zola," he used to call them.
I contended that I was a "cultural provocateur." The covers outraged the mighty,
angered advertisers, and infuriated readers–but they visualized
the changes in America and needled our hypocrisies. And Harold never
let anyone or anything diddle with the work. The ruder
the raspberry, the happier was Hayes. That time is called the "Golden Age"
of magazine journalism, the birth of the "New Journalism."
Because it was *Harold's* time! Harold addressed the torrid issues of race, war,
and politics. He blasted the silly pretensions of pop culture
and deflated the synthetic images of celebrities. His *Esquire*, always
on the cutting edge of cultural awareness, owed something
to the times–but the times owed something to *Esquire*! People ask
me all the time why there aren't any more great magazine
covers like *Esquire*'s. I tell them because there aren't any more buccaneering
bad boys like Harold Hayes. That courageous North Carolina
country boy nailed down that messy, turbulent decade, and his brave work
will remain the toughest antidote to revisionist historians.
Long may my remarkable pal, Harold Hayes, be remembered. ■

Esquire
THE MAGAZINE FOR MEN
JULY 1965
PRICE 75¢
Does today's teen-ager influence the adult world?
"Ridiculous,"
says Ed Sullivan.
Esquire
COLLEGE ISSUE
SEPTEMBER 1966
PRICE 75¢
THE MAGAZINE FOR MEN
How our red blooded
campus heroes
are beating the draft:

In this reprint from Esquire's *Editor Page, September 1972, Harold Hayes muses over the decade we worked together. Six months later, Hayes quit* Esquire, *and I quit doing* Esquire *covers. Circulation had risen from 500,000 to almost 2,000,000.*

THE TRIALS AND TRIUMPHS OF A DECADE WORKING WITH GEORGE LOIS

Breakfast last Tuesday at the Park Lane to discuss with George Lois the cover for next month's issue. Uncharacteristically, he showed up about eight minutes late, apologizing because his earlier meeting had run long. Earlier by how much, I asked. What time had it begun? "Six," George said without flinching. To mind came a blackout from *New Faces of 1952* in which a jazz musician is hauled into court for disturbing the peace. "We was just having a little party in my flat on Saturday night, your honor," the musician says. "Yes, well, when did the party end?" the judge asks. The musician grins, stomps on the floor, and cries, *"Thursday!"* Lois' delivery is more casual. He does not expect the world to set its watch by his work schedules; on the other hand, if it doesn't, he sees no reason why it should get in his way.

George Lois is a tough and loving Greek, an advertising man, and an amateur basketball player, roughly in that order.

Next month he will publish an autobiography of a sort, *George, be careful*, and at the same time mark his tenth year of producing *Esquire*'s covers—a lively period during which he has persuaded Andy Warhol to jump into a can of Campbell's soup, Roy Cohn to wear an angel's halo, Ed Sullivan a Beatles wig, mean Sonny Liston a Santa Claus hat, and a heterosexual to wear lipstick.

Lois himself never wears anything on his head, perhaps with good reason.

His talent is spread over many enterprises—his own advertising agency, a film production company, a design firm—yet his own artistry is instantly identifiable, his effort limitless, his attention to detail obsessively meticulous.

His sense of morality—a pertinent factor, since people constantly ask why we do those things we do on our covers—was formed in the house of his father, a florist in the Bronx, and in the streets outside. When he was twelve, a gang from another block came to his neighborhood and took off his pants. In an effort to subdue him, one of the members of the gang broke George's arm. He waited for months until his attacker returned to his neighborhood. "Then what did you do?," I asked him. "Then I followed him until he was alone and I broke his arm," Lois said.

The image of the soul-rotted adman, trembling before the wrath of his client in order to keep his ranch house in Westport, is not the image of George Lois.

George, be careful
A Greek florist's kid in the roughhouse world of advertising
George Lois with Bill Pitts

HARALAMPOS LOIS IN HIS COLUMBIA FLORIST SHOP IN THE BRONX, 1933

To destroy Lois it would first be necessary to shoot him through the heart
with a silver bullet, and then you couldn't be absolutely sure.
His visual excellence springs from two sources: a) his belief that a picture
is dependent upon some accompanying statement in order to project an idea;
b) his intuitive grasp of the idea to be rendered.
What is left unaccounted for within these parameters may be summarized as talent.
More than any other single element within this period—more than
The Confessions of Lieutenant Calley, the reporting of social and historical disasters,
the outrageousness of some of our titles—his covers for *Esquire*
have drawn fire because they have been considered either controversial,
or irreverent, or tasteless.
Yet in retrospect it is more often his critic whom time proves the fool.
In December of '63, the famous Liston Santa Claus portrait prophetically challenged
the illusions of racism.
In March of '65, Virna Lisi, lathered up and shaving before the camera,
signaled the sexist war soon to follow.

In November of '66, Hubert Humphrey was posed as a ventriloquist's dummy
on the knee of Lyndon Johnson.
A few months after the assassination of Robert Kennedy, homage was paid to Bobby,
brother John, and Dr. King, resurrected on the grounds of Arlington National
Cemetery. Lieutenant Calley smiling and surrounded by four Vietnamese children,
in November of 1970, sought to make the point that Calley's assumed lack
of guilt was a stupid innocence shared by us all.
A tough cover, but George had the full freedom we traditionally offered
our best talent. He has always signed his name to his covers, when I was able
to convince him, down there in the lower-left-hand corner, in four-point type.
So have we, with the standard *Esquire* script across the top.
And always with great enthusiasm on both our parts. It's hard to think who else
might better have expressed what this magazine is all about.
But trouble? Oh, Lord, the trouble he has caused.
Late one Sunday evening several months ago, I received a call from Harold Conrad, a fight
promoter who happened to be a friend of mine and of Norman Mailer's as well.
"Harold," growled the other Harold, "I had a card fall out on me for a promotion in Zurich.

I was up to Norman's house and he's into boxing now.
I asked him if he wanted to fight an exhibition match. He said he would if he could fight who he wanted, and he wants to fight you. How about it?"
Of the many byzantine objections developed by Mailer toward *Esquire* over the years, Lois' September cover of last year (1971) is doubtless among the most galling.
There was Mailer, montaged into a King Kong suit, tenderly cradling an ecstatic Germaine Greer—all provocatively arranged for the reader to consider Greer's response inside to Mailer's *The Prisoner of Sex*.
It was one of George's most inspired covers—Mailer, the king of machismo, as seen by one of the great graphic artists of our time.
On past occasions it has been noted here that the editor is really not much more than a surrogate reader, one who appreciates in advance the best of what is offered him to publish, the Mailers of our time, the Buckleys, the Vidals, the Hatfields and the McCoys.
His role is that of an honest broker, and in this case ol' George deserves all the credit.
So what the hell, I say; eliminate the middleman! Norman,
George can be found any morning in his office after 6 a.m., 688-1525.

HAROLD T.P. HAYES

HAROLD HAYES, 1965

THE MoMA ESQUIRE COLLECTION 1962–1972

CALLING A TITLE FIGHT ON MY FIRST MAGAZINE COVER

After hearing editor Harold Hayes' description of the collaborative process used to create *Esquire*'s covers, my exact Bronx-accented reaction was, "Holy shit, pal—group fucking grope! Just give it to one outside guy." Shaken, Southern-born Harold Hayes drawled, "Ol' buddy, could y'all do me just *one* cover—'cause I dunno what the hell y'all talkin' about!" I accepted the challenge, and Hayes ticked off the lineup about to go to press. Amid the articles was a short piece on the upcoming world-championship heavyweight bout between the champion, Floyd Patterson, and his monster challenger, Sonny Liston. I decided to do a surrealistic piece on defeat, on how people treat a loser in the ring, in business, or in life. Harold Krieger photographed this scene in the spooky St. Nicholas Arena on West 66th Street just a few weeks before it was razed. I used a black model who was built like Patterson, who was rated a 5 to 1 favorite to retain his championship. There wasn't a bookmaker in Vegas who gave Liston a chance to outpoint Patterson, but I just *knew* he'd coldcock Floyd. The cover called for a loser, and if I could, I wanted to be accurate by choosing the appropriate Everlast trunks (the champ's choice). But Cus D'Amato, Patterson's manager, wouldn't tell me which Floyd would wear. So we shot the scene twice, first with black trunks, then with white. But we were forced to take a guess at what the champ would wear. So I asked Harold Hayes to flip a coin. The black trunks won, and *Esquire* ran it. A few weeks later, after my first cover appeared, Liston demolished Patterson in the first round! The punched-out champ fell to the canvas in *black* Everlasts. (I lucked out again.) The press wrote about the chutzpah of calling a fight on a magazine cover, and the issue was a sellout. I may have called the fight, but I also showed what losing meant in our tough world: being left for dead.
Nobody loves a loser.

P.S. In 1962, when my first cover ran, *Esquire* was deeply in the red.
A few years later, it was knocking down millions in profit.

LAST MAN IN THE RING: SONNY LISTON AND FLOYD PATTERSON TALK ABOUT BEING TOUGH AND SCARED

MY EARLY-WARNING SIGNAL OF A BAD WAR

Editor Harold Hayes and I only debated two covers I created for him. The first was this early-warning signal on Vietnam. In the fall of 1962, I sent this mock-up to Harold. I wanted to use the actual 100th G.I. who had lost his life in 'Nam, but the U.S. State Department refused. So I dusted off a Korean War snapshot of me (when I was in Japan on R&R), hoping the power of *Esquire* could force the Defense Department to release the actual photo of the G.I. In those days, Vietnam was considered a minor fracas. "It'll be over by Christmas" was the war cry. Since *Esquire* covers had to be prepared two months in advance, Harold was afraid we might end up with egg on our face. So, very reluctantly, I killed my "100th G.I." cover. By the time we evacuated Vietnam almost 13 years later, with our tails between our legs, more than 58,000 American G.I.'s had been killed or were missing in action.

The only other rejected cover was for a 1968 "Black Rage" issue Harold was planning on a militant black movement (the Black Panthers among them) that was frightening even the left-wingers who had fought many years against racial injustice in America. I enlarged the original logo of Aunt Jemima pancakes, and created an image showing her wearing a Black Panther beret and wielding a cleaver (a reference to the volatile Eldridge Cleaver). I knew the visual would infuriate the white establishment in America, because I was saying that the pre-'60s "mammy" image many whites had of subservient blacks had been transformed into that of a defiant, violent, black revolutionary. A vengeful Aunt Jemima lurking in millions of America's kitchens scared the hell out of Harold, enough to make me throw it out.

MY PROPOSED "BLACK RAGE" COVER IMAGE THAT SCARED THE HELL OUT OF HAROLD HAYES (AND WOULD SURELY HAVE SHOCKED AMERICA IN 1968).

PRICE $1.50
Esquire
THE MAGAZINE FOR MEN
"Merry Christmas.
I'm the
100th G.I. killed
in Vietnam."

THE NEW MORALITY

At the birth of a decade of a rapidly changing American culture,
Esquire caught a whiff of the new sexual ground rules for the '60s:
1. No more stigma to illegitimacy.
2. No more traditional marriages in American society.
My cover crystallized this new, complicated mix of women's
emancipated attitudes, aggressive sexual liberation,
and the extinction of the double standard. To condense it all,
we showed this triumphant bride surrounded by
no less than eight "love-children" and one dumbstruck husband.
(The models were an ethnic Greek-American couple
with two kids of their own, three of my nephews,
two nieces, and my four-year-old son, Harry Joe—the one sitting
closest to the beaming mama.) Take another look
and you'll see how this deceptively innocent image proclaims
that common-law marriages were out of the closet
and the sexual revolution was here to stay.
Appropriately, I gave Timothy Galfas, a fellow Greek-American,
the honor of photographing this wedding portrait.

JUST MARRIED!? FOR MORE ON LOVE (AND A TOUCH OF SIN) SEE PAGE 83

THE PROMISE OF THE '60s

In those faraway Kennedy years, when all seemed possible, Gore Vidal twitted Americans about what to many seemed inevitable: that after Jack served his own eight triumphant years, the firebrand brother he'd anointed attorney general would ascend to that seat in the Oval Office. Even after the assassination of JFK, eight months later, and the presidency of Lyndon Johnson, Vidal was on the nose with his prediction, until the fateful night of Robert Kennedy's assassination, on June 6, 1968, on his destined march to the presidency. It was an American tragedy, because Bobby just looked so *right* in Jack's rocker!

MARCH 1963
PRICE 60¢

Esquire

THE MAGAZINE FOR MEN

GORE VIDAL CHOOSES THE BEST MAN, 1968...

CALIFORNIA DREAMIN'

This salacious cover, obviously created before the attack of the feminist bra-burners, made two points:
1. You can't believe everything you see, especially in the fake, opportunistic ambience of La-La Land...
2. *Esquire*, even while deeply immersed in the "New Journalism," wasn't averse to flashing a little of its own pre-Madonna pointy T and A. Boys will be boys.

MAY 1963
PRICE 60c

Esquire

THE MAGAZINE FOR MEN

TRUE AND FALSE VALUES IN THE STATE OF CALIFORNIA

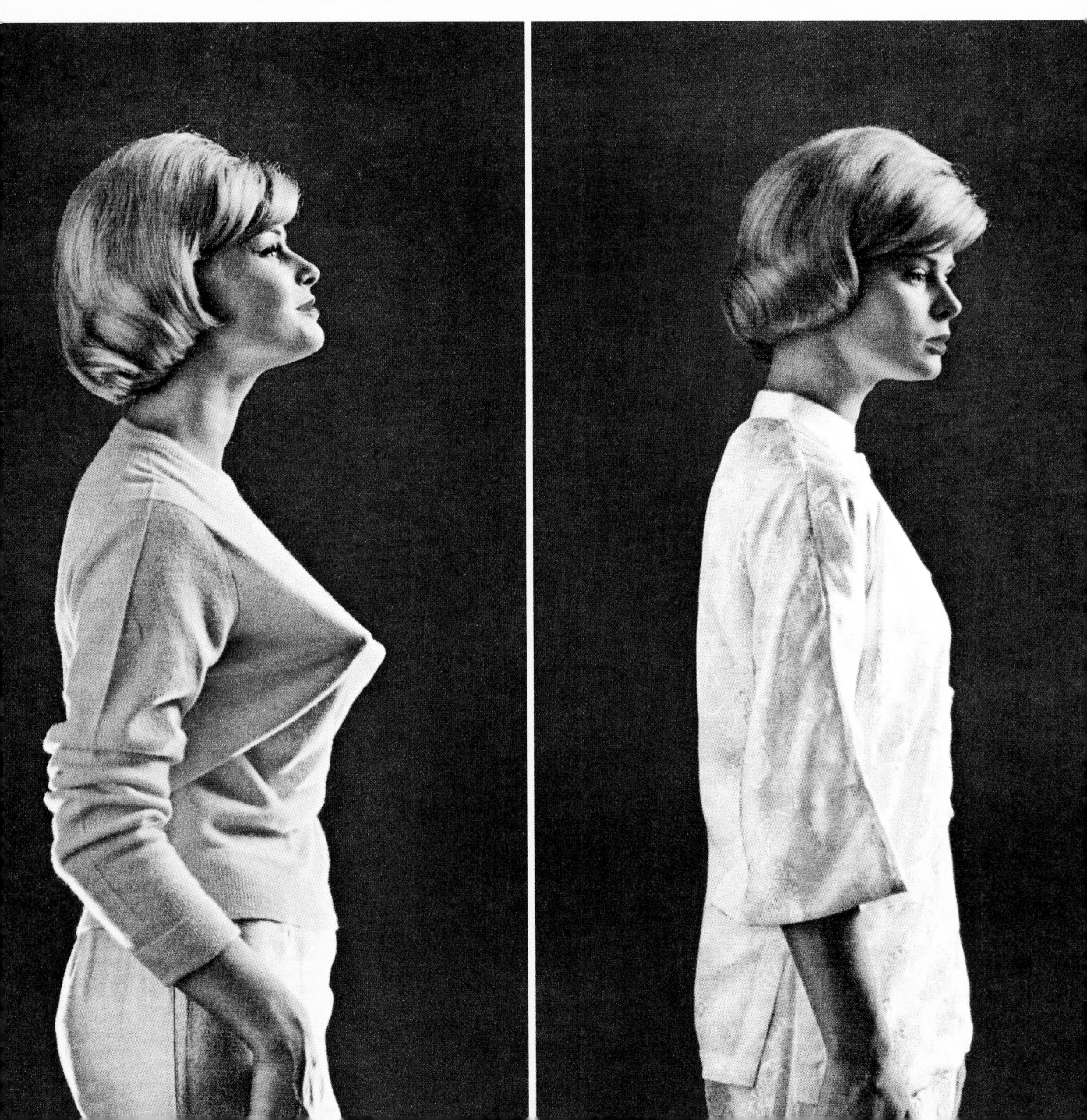

UNCLE SAM AS ANTIHERO

After the military folly known as the Bay of Pigs Invasion, a shaken
but wiser President Kennedy showed new steel. He powerfully
and painstakingly maneuvered the Soviet premier Nikita Khrushchev into
packing up his nuclear missiles and sailing back to Moscow.
The Cuban Missile Crisis scared the hell out of America, especially
us prime-target New Yorkers. In our nation's capital,
murderous plots against Fidel Castro kept the lights burning until
the wee hours. That was the atmosphere around this 1963
cover of a real-life, vengeful Uncle Sam exhorting America to overthrow
the revolutionary populist government that had overthrown
the corrupt and despotic Fulgencio Batista. Predictably, it infuriated
the top brass at the Pentagon. They denied, but could not
squelch, the hot, persistent rumors of secret C.I.A. hit squads conspiring
against Fidel. When my Uncle Sam whipped up the flames,
semper fi marine lieutenant Harold Hayes was bombarded with telephone
death threats, all in thick Cuban accents. Hayes didn't dare
inform his bosses of the threats, for fear management would chicken out
when he next went over the editorial edge. He also swore me to
secrecy. By transforming the great (and patriotic) James Montgomery Flagg's
World War I poster, changing an altruistic Uncle Sam into a symbol
of American colonial arrogance, we sent out a signal. The cover helped set
the political tone and attitude of *Esquire* for years to come.
Five short months later, not Castro but JFK was shot to death.
Makes you think.

JUNE 1963
PRICE 60¢
Esquire
THE MAGAZINE FOR MEN

JOIN UP
FOR THE
MARCH
THROUGH
HAVANA
THE C.I.A.
WANTS YOU
FOR FURTHER RECRUITING INFORMATION SEE INSIDE

CLEOPATRA'S ENORMOUS CLEAVAGE

Cleopatra was a $40 million production—the most expensive movie ever made at that time. During its filming, the steamy affair between Richard Burton and Elizabeth Taylor (while hubby Eddie Fisher was growing horns) was a worldwide sensation. For the August 1963 issue *Esquire* ran a long piece on the stars' open romancing on the set. The hotter their affair, the better for *Cleopatra*'s box office (or so the producers hoped). A few days before the cover deadline, my wife, Rosie, was riding down Broadway in a cab with my son Harry Joe, and spotted a gigantic *Cleopatra* poster being painted over the Rivoli Theatre, where the movie was to premiere. She jumped out of the cab and into a pay phone, called me at my office, and described the almost surrealistic scene to me. It was an *Esquire* cover in the making if I could get the shot in time. I hightailed it down to 49th Street, saw it, ran across the street, rented a hotel room on the sixth floor facing the Rivoli marquee, and called photographer Carl Fischer. The sign painters had already finished Liz's enormous breasts, so I slipped them a twenty to raise the scaffold and get back to the eye-popping focal point of that incredible real-life farce.

AUGUST 1963
PRICE 60c

Esquire

THE MAGAZINE FOR MEN

THE CLEOPATRA PAPERS. ABSOLUTELY, POSITIVELY, THE LAST WORD. NO KIDDING. P. 33

PAPERT KOENIG LOIS FIELDED CHAMPIONSHIP SEMI-PRO SOFTBALL AND BASKETBALL TEAMS DURING THE '60s. SHOWN HERE IS GEORGE LOIS IN 1963, A FEW YEARS AFTER LEAVING DOYLE DANE BERNBACH TO FOUND PKL, HITTING A HOME RUN AGAINST HIS ALMA MATER.

MY BIZARRE HARPER'S COVER

Esquire's editors took a swipe at *Vogue* and *Harper's Bazaar* by showing what truly goes on at a high-fashion shoot. As trusty as calendars, the great fashion models are time-markers of our fast-changing popular culture. When I staged this cover to symbolize real versus imagined glamour, Jean Shrimpton, with her fresh '60s look, was replacing the haughty Suzy Parker as the new haute couture glamourpuss (with Twiggy foreshadowing the coming of Kate Moss, sullen waif of the '90s). As expected, both Parker and Shrimpton were appalled by my debunking concept for an *Esquire* cover. In those days, these storklike mannequins, armed with designer creations, lacquered nails, ruby lips, and nylon-smooth legs up to their shoulders, were not famous for their sense of humor. But Dolores Wettach, a beauty with a mind (and brains) of her own, ignored the advice of her mentors at the Ford Model Agency. She dug out her grungiest jeans and sneakers, belted down a Pepsi, took a drag on her Benson & Hedges, hunkered down on some milk crates, and looked magnificent for fashion photographer Art Kane's camera.

OCTOBER, 1963
PRICE 60c

Esquire

THE MAGAZINE FOR MEN

INSIDE THE SQUARE: GLAMOR. OUTSIDE: REAL LIFE. TO LEARN THE DIFFERENCE, SEE PAGE 125

THE FIRST BLACK SANTA

Sonny Liston was perfect for the part. By now he was known by everyone as the meanest man in the world. He was a sullen and surly champion, a real badass. He had served time for armed robbery and didn't give a damn about his image. This newest heavyweight champion of the world flaunted his menacing image at a time when rising racial fever dominated the headlines. The early '60s were the years of Freedom Rides, Dr. Martin Luther King, Jr., black revolution, and rising racial tensions. I was looking into the eyes of a changing America. I explained the idea of a black Santa to Liston's adviser and idol, Joe Louis. "That'll be the day," said Joe skeptically, but he went ahead and twisted Sonny's arm, and we captured an image on film of the Western World's newest Santa. All hell broke loose when the cover came out. Several advertisers took their money and ran. Subscribers demanded refunds. Angry letters flowed in. Harold Hayes loved the cover but admitted that Sonny Liston created more trouble than any cover since the invention of movable type. Eighteen years later, recalling the era, *Sports Illustrated* said, "Four months after Liston won the title, *Esquire* thumbed its nose at its white readers with an unforgettable cover. On the front of its December 1963 issue, there was Liston glowering out from under a tasseled red-and-white Santa Claus hat, looking like the last man on earth America wanted to see coming down its chimney." And *Time* magazine described the cover as "one of the greatest social statements of the plastic arts since Picasso's *Guernica*." Ho, ho, ho.

P.S. A few years later, when I paired a dead-eyed Sonny Liston sitting next to a loquacious Andy Warhol on a Braniff International TV spot, I asked Liston what his reaction was when the notorious cover hit the newsstands, pissing off every white person in America. "Well-l-l, my *kids* loved it," he muttered, almost sweetly.

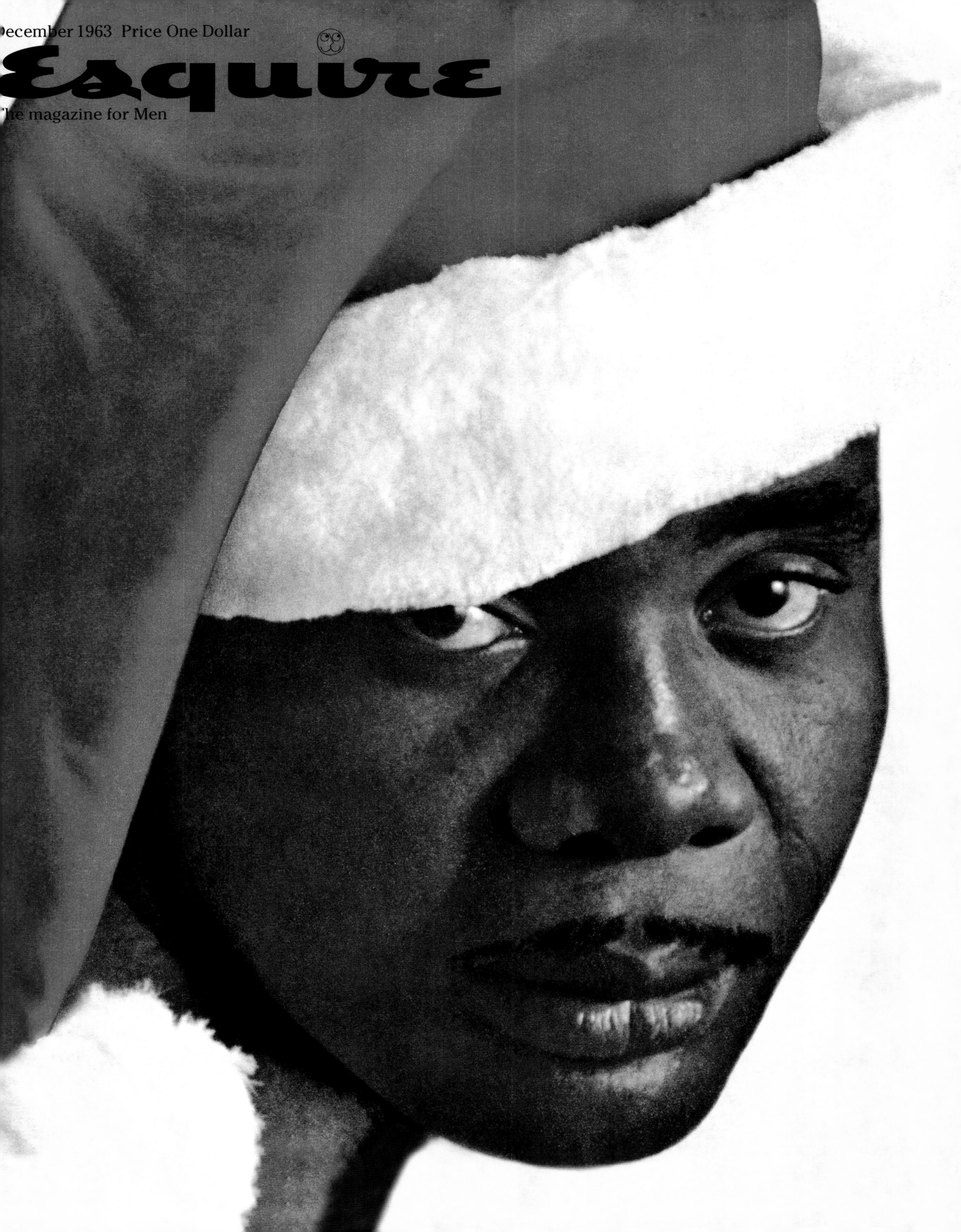

ecember 1963 Price One Dollar
Esquire
he magazine for Men

THE COVER THAT TOOK OFF

To make up for my refusal to create the typical *Esquire* "cover girl" cover that American men had come to expect since 1933, I went whole hog with a complete beauty pageant on a 10 x 12 5/8 inch magazine cover. The feature story dealt with travel, so I invited 15 of the top international airlines in the world to send me their hottest stewardesses. In those Neanderthal days you had to be young and a knockout in stiletto heels to work the aisles. The 40 working girls had a good time, and photographer Timothy Galfas and I had an eyeful, as we served cheesecake and coffee, tea, or milk all around. Inexplicably, it became one of *Esquire*'s biggest-selling issues on the newsstands. Men, I swear, were actually choosing their overseas airlines by the women on that cover!

Fly to Europe with the stewardess of your choice. On the way, read p.69

Ettie Housman, El Al
Eliane Gottlieb, Air France
Nicole Savoye, Air France
Zarine Vakil, Air India
Pushpa Nargolwala, Air India
Krishnat Mahtani, Air India
Nily Eisner, El Al
Runa Brynjolfsdottir, Icelandic
9 Hildur Hauksdottir, Icelandic
10 Stefania Gudmundsdottir, Icelandic
11 Jill Wolff, BOAC
12 Helen D'Aquino, BOAC
13 Sherry Wing, BOAC
14 Albertina Castellani, Alitalia
15 Maria Monteforte, Alitalia
16 Marie Aspland, TWA
17 Joan Honold, TWA
18 Karin Krahmer, Lufthansa
19 Lillian Frizzole, Pan American
20 May Yasuda, Pan American
21 Jill Edwards, SAS
22 Carlotta Gunther, Alitalia
23 Rose Marie Maisonet, Iberia
24 Mary Lynn McCutcheon, TWA
25 Patricia Price, TWA
26 Bonnie Friesth, TWA
27 Helga Schenk, Lufthansa
28 Barbara Brennan, Pan American
29 Karin Weber, Pan American
30 Anita Appelgren, SAS
31 Irene Hval, SAS
32 Sheila Hansen, Irish Intl. Airlines
33 Una Madden, Irish Intl. Airlines
34 Thérèse Maton, Sabena
35 Danièle Vuylsteke, Sabena
36 Karin Steidle, Lufthansa
37 Barbara Keller, Qantas
38 Annette Carswell, Pan American
39 Doris Hegnauer, Swissair
40 Marlen Menzi, Swissair

THE INDIAN NICKEL FLIES MOHAWK

I spotted an article on the American Indian in the advance draft of the March 1964 *Esquire* issue. On a lark, I phoned the Bureau of Indian Affairs in Washington, D.C. to find out if they had the remotest notion as to what Native American posed for the Indian Head/Buffalo nickel, and if he might still be alive! I felt that I was on the verge of a major historical find, especially when the Washington paleface called back and stammered on the phone in shock, “His name was, I mean is Chief John Big Tree… He m-m-may still be alive… if so, he should be on his Onondaga Reservation.” My father-in-law, Joe Lewandowski, a Syracusan, completed my research. He drove out to the reservation, where he found Chief John Big Tree in the flesh, toting twigs to light a fire in his primitive, dirt-floor cabin. He was a vigorous 87 years old and stood six feet two. I couldn’t wait to catch the first plane up there, but Chief John loved to fly. He showed up at Carl Fischer’s studio in a business suit, sporting a crewcut. In 1912, the sculptor James Earle Fraser had spotted the chief in a Coney Island Wild West show and asked him to pose for his Indian Head nickel, destined to become the greatest coin designed since ancient Greece. The chief was a Seneca, a descendant of the Iroquois Confederacy, which dates back to the 1500s. At the shoot, we dressed him in a black wig and built up his toothless mouth with cotton wads. He looked awesome. We shot his historic profile, and he flew back to Syracuse on Mohawk Airlines. It was vintage Americana—the legendary Chief John Big Tree a half-century after he posed for the Indian Head/Buffalo nickel! After his noble profile hit the newsstands, he was recruited on the TV talk-show circuit, and the unknown chief became a heroic, iconic celebrity.

MARCH 1964
PRICE 60¢

Esquire

THE MAGAZINE FOR MEN

Good Indians we got (page 58). Bad Indians you can have (page 76).

Chief Johnny Big Tree, today... and as he looked when he posed for the Indian-head nickel 51 years ago:

PHOOEY ON THE 1964 WORLD'S FAIR

Inside this issue, *Esquire* welcomed the 1964-1965 New York World's Fair, brandishing its Unisphere, a big, skeletal metal globe that looked like the world had imploded. But to me there was only *one* fair. A fantasy of showmanship, the epitome of stagecraft, a real-life Land of Oz, the 1939-1940 New York World's Fair had become indelibly etched in the memories of all who attended. Born of national tragedy, it signaled the end of the Great Depression and reflected our boundless belief in the "World of Tomorrow." The Trylon and Perisphere, an enormous white, futuristic temple, became the fair's centerpiece, architectural symbol, and visual logo. Designed by Wallace Harrison and André Fouilhoux, it symbolized a beacon of hope that had endured one storm of conflict (as we were about to enter another). It remains the stuff of memories! This thinking man's cover, using that memorable and beautiful symbol of the 1939 fair, with nostalgic references to the original, to the *real* fair, said phooey to the '64 fair! (And double phooey to its phony slogan: "Peace Through Understanding.") Read my captions very carefully. If you're too young to decipher them, ask your grandfather.

April 1964, price 60¢

Esquire

Exclusive! A flashback guide to the best World's Fair ever.

"They say by 1960, the
sidewalks will be
20 feet above the roads.
Aah, we'll all own autogiros
by then, anyway."

"Guess who we saw
at the Aquacade.
Cary Grant.
He still looks nifty
and I'll bet he's forty."

"If you want to
relax for a minute,
go see the Japanese Pavilion.
It's so peaceful."

"Look, I didn't drive 800 miles
just to see
Elsie the Cow. I want to get
a World's Fair penny."

"How can Grover Whelan
run this whole Fair
and remain such a nice guy.
Holy Moses!"

A NATION'S TEARS

Kennedy Without Tears was a June 1964
article by Tom Wicker that looked at JFK "objectively,"
seven months after the assassination.
My trompe l'oeil cover showed the opposite symbolism—
of Kennedy himself, crying for his lost destiny.
(Or are they, after all, the tears of the reader?)
For most Americans, the murder
of our president was an unrelieved trauma.
Nerves were apparently as raw in June
as they had been in November.
Even though the issue was a big seller, I caught hell
from a lot of people for being "insensitive."
But this cover still brings a tear to my eyes.

JUNE 1964
PRICE 60c
Esquire
THE MAGAZINE FOR MEN
Kennedy without tears.
See page 108

LIZ KISSES-OFF THE MEDIA

Cuckolding Eddie Fisher on the world's front pages, Liz Cleopatra'd her way down the Nile with Richard Burton (see page 50). After doing everything else with him, she married the raucous, hard-drinking Welshman. Elizabeth Taylor proved, over and over again, that she never went to bed with a man she didn't end up marrying. The media had its tasteless field day, and never let up. Liz swore off interviews and photo shoots as every magazine in the world hounded her. I took it as a challenge to somehow con her into an *Esquire* cover story. But how could I possibly entice her? I had a sweet, motherly idea! I knew that Timothy Galfas, the great Hollywood cinematographer, TV commercial director, and photographer, could come to the rescue, so I asked him if he could help me coax Mrs. Burton to let us photograph her for a surprise pullout cover—she would reveal that her "greatest love" was (heh-heh) her young daughter, Liza (whose daddy was Mike Todd, Taylor's third husband). In Galfas' entrapping Southern drawl and my Noo Yawk accent, we convinced her that she'd come off as a feisty good sport, and at the same time she'd tell the media world to kiss-off. Galfas photographed her lushly, and the issue became a giant newsstand seller.

TURN THE PAGE
TO SEE
ELIZABETH TAYLOR'S
GREATEST LOVE:

THIS IS LIZA
SEE PAGE 118

GEORGE LOIS DIRECTING AN ESQUIRE *SHOOT WITH PHOTOGRAPHER TIMOTHY GALFAS, 1964.*

A CHEEKY COVER ON THE APPROACHING WOMEN'S MOVEMENT

The year 1965 was pre-Betty Friedan, pre-Gloria Steinem, pre-Bella Abzug. For an article on the masculinization of the American woman, just as the hoopla about the women's movement had caught the public's eye, I wanted to do a spoof of a movie star caught in a manly act. The budding movement wanted liberation from women's traditional roles. Like any Greek male, I wondered where it would take us. The best way to draw attention to a trend on the horizon in the '60s was a cutting-edge *Esquire* cover on the approaching confusion between the sexes. But in those uptight days, I was turned down by every American beauty queen in Hollywood, including Kim Novak, Marilyn Monroe, and Jayne Mansfield. Then Virna Lisi, the *molto bellissima* actress, about to debut in America in the film *How to Murder Your Wife*, co-starring Jack Lemmon, recognized the humor of the manly pose, had the machismo to flaunt her beauty, and lathered up. The Italian knockout, a knockoff of the German Marlene Dietrich, laughed with gusto and took it off on the front cover of America's leading men's magazine.

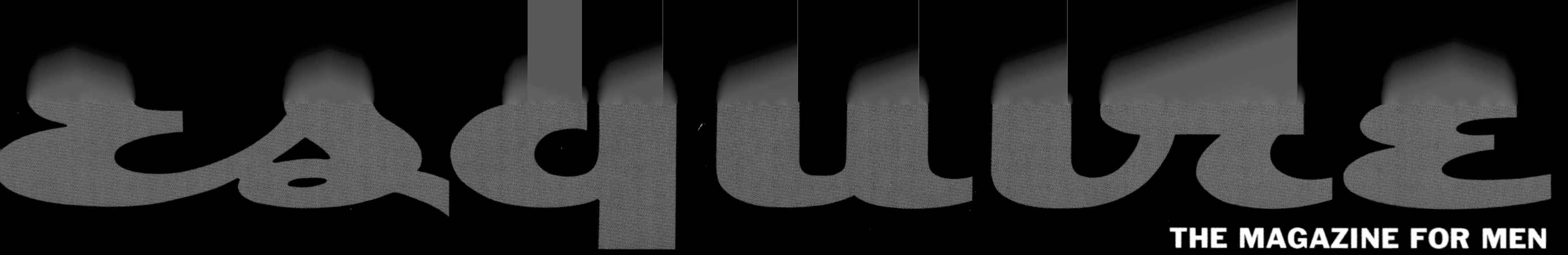

THE MAGAZINE FOR MEN

The masculinization of the American woman. See page 76

"THAT'S OUR HITLER!"

It was the 20th anniversary of the day the 56-year-old
Adolf Hitler blew his maniacal brains out.
Yet a pollster had found that almost half of all Americans
believed he had bamboozled the avenging
Russian army. They were convinced that he had spirited himself
out of his Berlin bunker into the arms of a loving,
loyal Argentina. By the '60s, neo-Nazism was rearing its
appalling head in Germany—and even in America.
Resigned to the brutal fact that fascism and anti-Semitism
had never died, I reincarnated the leader of the
Third Reich, emerging from the shadows of exile, pleading
for redemption. Photographer Harold Krieger
and I searched, vainly, for exactly the unfortunate face that
could double as der Führer. Eerily, we encountered
him in a German beer hall in Manhattan's Yorkville. Before
World War II, Yorkville crawled with pro-Nazi
brownshirts of the German-American Bund. As he sat there,
beckoning for another stein of beer with a
flawless Nazi salute, I turned to Harold and exclaimed,
"That's our Hitler!"

P.S. Three years later, in Mel Brooks' original film production of
The Producers, in an audition for their leading man,
Max Bialystock (Zero Mostel) spots the looniest choice possible and
screams to Leo Bloom (Gene Wilder), "That's our Hitler!"
Déjà vu all over again.

MAY, 1965
PRICE 75c

Esquire

THE MAGAZINE FOR MEN

"This month I will be 76 years old. Can I come home now?"
(See page 114, Adolf)

ED SULLIVAN WIGS OUT

Watching the showman Ed Sullivan introduce Beatlemania to America
on his Sunday-night TV variety show, I knew *Esquire*
had to acknowledge this establishment elder, with his uncanny
knack for being on the cutting edge of popular culture
(even though he'd kept his cameras off the pelvis of Elvis eight years before).
The Liverpool Fab Four with their outrageous bowl cuts
had landed, and they would soon reach the apex of pop music.
So, that Monday morning, I tried to go through the channels
at CBS and ask the impresario to pose – in a Beatles wig! My first job
as a Korean War vet was at CBS, working for the all-powerful
imagemaker, Bill Golden, the creator of the CBS eye. And I knew
my old boss Bill Paley, the chairman of CBS, was a fan of
my *Esquire* covers. But Paley brushed me off, suspicious of what effect
the imagery of that really big showman wearing a Beatles wig
would have. So I decided to amble over to The Ed Sullivan Theater
(where David Letterman now cavorts) and camp at the
entrance, right there on Broadway. When Sullivan finally came out,
I shoved a sketch of my proposed *Esquire* cover in his face
and talked fast. He took a long look and grinned from ear to ear,
just like the final shot we took the next day.
He wore his wig with gusto and smiled like Ringo.

Esquire
THE MAGAZINE FOR MEN
JULY 1965
PRICE 75¢
Does today's teen-ager
influence the adult world?
"Ridiculous,"
says Ed Sullivan.

THE FACE OF A HERO THAT INFURIATED AMERICA

This *Esquire* cover incensed the establishment—but in 1965 the college students of America embraced this composite of the men I chose as the leading heroes of American youth. Four inspirational revolutionaries—Bob Dylan, Malcolm X, Fidel Castro, and President John F. Kennedy—are divided (and joined) by the crosshairs of a rifle sight. Kennedy and Malcolm had been murdered, and Castro (we now know) escaped several assassination attempts and is still regarded by many (including me) as a romantic revolutionary. The poet Dylan continued to compose and sing of that violent, revolting age. (Today, alas, without heroes, we must make do with celebrities.)

4 of the 28 who count most with the college rebels:

(for the others see page 97)

GODS AND GLADIATORS

This cover image kicked off an *Esquire* issue crammed full of exhilarating sportswriting. Instead of a sports action cover, we photographed Darrell Dess, a pugnacious New York Giants guard, in the mood of a Renaissance painting, praying for survival. Back then, a professional athlete praying on his knees was a sight gag. My joke in 1965 has become a reality. In today's game, born-again Christians preach to teammates, opponents, fans, the media, and anyone within earshot that the only way to heaven is through Jesus, insisting that those who aren't Christians are doomed to hell. This bigotry towards Jews, Buddhists, Muslims, and agnostics has divided many a locker room in America. In his second inaugural address, meditating on the paradoxes of the Civil War, Abraham Lincoln, the greatest moral leader in the Western world since Jesus Christ, intoned: "Both read the same Bible and pray to the same God, and each invokes His aid against the other." The idea of a God who is a Giants fan—or an Eagles fan, or a Patriots fan, or a Redskins fan—is ludicrous. If there *is* a God who watches NFL football on Sunday afternoons and Monday nights and gives a damn, while ignoring the millions of starving children in the world, we're all in hell *now.*

OCTOBER 1965
PRICE 75¢

Esquire

THE MAGAZINE FOR MEN

Heaven help him – he's going to play 60 minutes of pro ball

SIR LANCELOT HE'S NOT

Lyndon Johnson, thrust into the presidency by Lee Harvey Oswald, tried to carve out his own greatness with his proclamation of America's Great Society. To help win the South, Jack Kennedy had cynically enlisted the garrulous Texan as his running mate in 1960, then buried ambitious LBJ in traditional and inane VP duties with the blessing of baby-brother Robert, his hard-charging attorney general. The promise of Camelot pervaded the White House of John F. Kennedy and his ethereal first lady. When it all turned to dust on November 22, 1963, the crude, shit-kicking Texan and his low-flying Lady Bird moved into the nation's first home. Compared with the royally stylish young Jack and Jackie, Lyndon and Lady Bird were hopelessly outclassed. Stuffing Lyndon's sour puss inside a gleaming Sir Lancelot getup made him look as foolish as I had hoped. A year before this cover, I had done Robert Kennedy's New York senatorial campaign. We had blunted the "carpetbagger" charges against Bobby and dramatized his energy and humaneness. Even so, I had pre-election fears, so in the last two weeks, as Johnson's campaign against the extremist Barry Goldwater caught fire, I convinced Bobby to sign off our TV spots with: *Get on the Johnson, Humphrey, Kennedy Team*, hoping the "party line" ploy would bring even those Democrats who didn't like Bobby into the fold. After winning handily, Bobby hated Johnson's guts more than ever. I don't think he ever forgave me (and maybe himself) for garnering those last-minute coattail votes. Long after the election, and the day this cover hit the newsstands, I was having lunch in the pool room at The Four Seasons when a bottle of Château Mouton Rothschild arrived at my table. The note read:
Dear George,
I see you finally got off the Johnson -Humphrey team.
Love the Esquire *cover*
Looking across the pool to spot the donor, I saw Senator Bobby rabbit-grinning at me.

NOVEMBER 1965
PRICE 75¢

Esquire

THE MAGAZINE FOR MEN

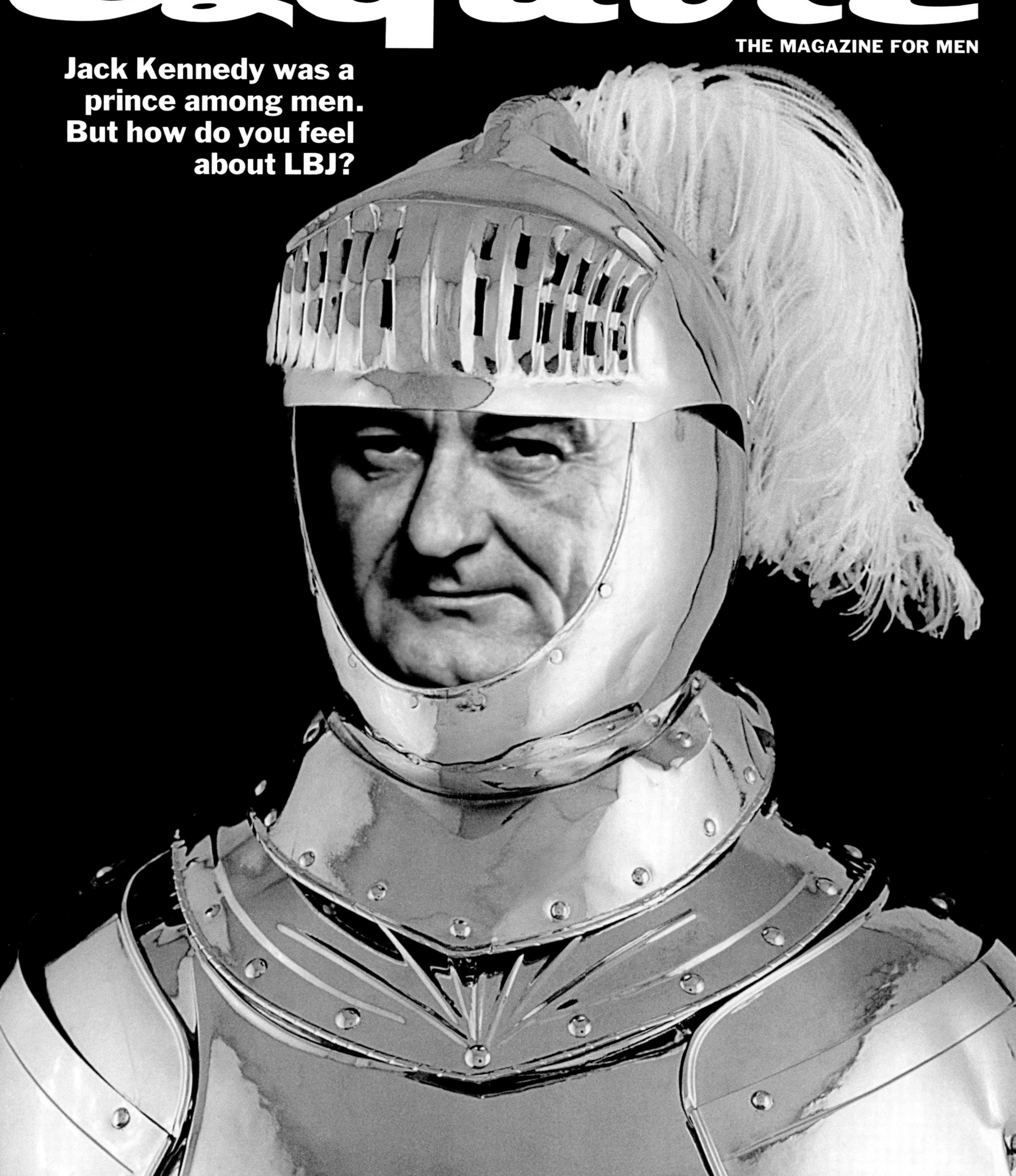

SINATRA AND HIS SICKO-PHANTS

Editor Harold Hayes dispatched Gay Talese, one of his brilliant young finds, to pursue Frank Sinatra and write a tough piece on the Chairman of the Board's power in the pop-music world, Hollywood, Las Vegas, and Washington. When the icon wouldn't grant him access for an interview, Talese profiled Sinatra's *entourage* (including "the little woman who carried Sinatra's hairpieces in a satchel"). His title *Frank Sinatra Has a Cold* inspired this cover on the brownnosing sicko-phants who light up the world of celebrities. The honor of one of my few illustrated covers for *Esquire* went to my talented buddy Edward Sorel, who nailed it. Word got back to *Esquire* that Ol' Blue Eyes was plenty burnt. (In 1970, when Sinatra graciously posed, gratis, for me in an Off-Track Betting *New York Bets* ad, I did *not* volunteer that I was responsible for this kiss-ass 1966 *Esquire* cover that he was reported to have detested.)

APRIL 1966
PRICE 75¢
Esquire
THE MAGAZINE
FOR MEN
The problems
of power
for Frank Sinatra
Edward Sorel

FAMOUS PEOPLE BEYOND REPROACH

The '60s were a time when Americans were becoming suspicious of celebrities, politicians, even their sports heroes. From a balcony above these "Unknockables" (clockwise from top: Kate Smith, John Cameron Swayze, Helen Hayes, Norman Thomas, Marianne Moore, Jimmy Durante, Eddie Bracken, and the center of their attention, the iconic Joe Louis), Carl Fischer asked them to look up at his camera. Norman Thomas was suffering from painful spinal paralysis and couldn't move his neck. Joe Louis leaned over and said gently to the old socialist, "Oh, Mr. Thomas, you never had trouble sticking your neck out before." Miraculously, Norman Thomas looked up and the camera saw the whites of his eyes.

JUNE 1966
PRICE 75c

THE MAGAZINE FOR MEN

n a time when everybody hates somebody—nobody hates

The Unknockables

Joe Louis
Marianne Moore
Norman Thomas
Helen Hayes
John Cameron Swayze
Kate Smith
Eddie Bracken
Jimmy Durante

42 others on page 84

WHEN THE GRADUATE WAS STILL A SOPHOMORE

The great Joltin' Joe DiMaggio, always a private person but always
with an eye for the ladies, came out of hiding when
he surprised the world by marrying the ultravisible Marilyn Monroe,
Hollywood's sex goddess. As a husband, he modestly
ducked behind her voluptuous curves and out of the limelight.
Too proud, classy, and important to become "Mr. Monroe,"
he and Marilyn split and the Yankee Clipper was out of sight again.
This cover hauntingly reflected on his absence (inspired
by yet another classic Gay Talese profile). Carl Fischer caught this
dreamlike apparition of Joe in one of his tailored civilian suits,
frozen at the apex of the most classic swing in the history of the game,
hitting one into the empty stands—a tiny lone figure in a hushed
cathedral. I almost asked No. 5 himself to pose, but even I don't have
that kind of hubris! So I cast dozens of lithe, athletic
51-year-old men but finally chose a 35-year-old who, as a kid,
had worshipped the ground Joe D. walked on: *moi*.
One year later, *Mrs. Robinson*, the theme song by Simon & Garfunkel for the
hit movie *The Graduate*, sported a lyric evoking all the nostalgia of our time:
Where have you gone, Joe DiMaggio?
A nation turns its lonely eyes to you (Ooo ooo ooo).
What's that you say, Mrs. Robinson?
Joltin' Joe has left and gone away (Hey hey hey, hey hey hey).

JULY 1966
PRICE 75c
Esquire
THE MAGAZINE FOR MEN
What's DiMaggio doing
with himself these days?
(see page 41)
SEC 11
SEC 9

THE FIRST OF THREE ESQUIRE COVERS IN DEFENSE OF "CASSIUS CLAY"

After defeating Sonny Liston in 1964, the new champion, who was then known by his Kentucky slave name, Cassius Marcellus Clay, announced to the world that he had become a Muslim, changing his name to Muhammad Ali. Before a November 1965 championship bout, Floyd Patterson foolishly taunted Ali by continually referring to him as "Cassius Clay." To avenge this disrespect for his religion, Ali vowed he would not only beat Patterson, he would "whup" him. And so he did. He held up the near-unconscious Patterson, punctuating blow after crippling blow with the mantra "What's my name! What's my name!" until, in the 12th round, he fell to the canvas—not merely beaten, but humiliated. Eight months later, knowing Floyd was a fair man and a good Christian, Harold Hayes and I convinced him to speak out in defense of the Muslim preacher. Ali was by then weathering a storm of controversy and was perceived as a draft dodger for refusing to fight in the Vietnam War. (Within a year, he was stripped of his title, and not allowed to fight for a living while waiting for his appeal to reach the U.S. Supreme Court.) When I called Floyd to make a date for a cover photo shoot with his tormentor, he agreed. But Patterson (who skulked around Brooklyn's Bedford-Stuyvesant streets wearing a beard as a disguise after losing face in 1959 by blowing a title bout to the "foreigner" Ingemar Johansson) insisted on a *midnight* shoot. No problem. I explained the cover idea (a preaching Patterson and a mute Ali) to a seemingly grateful Ali, begging him to receive Floyd with grace. Muhammad Ali was the first trash-talker in sports, and Floyd Patterson was the last gentleman in boxing. Ali was a sweetheart, but his biting tongue could have turned off the sensitive Patterson. At the stroke of midnight, almost cowering in a longshoreman's cap and a heavy overcoat (on a sweltering night in June), Floyd slipped into photographer Carl Fischer's studio. He saw Ali and froze in his tracks. Ali lovingly spread his arms, almost trotted up to Patterson, whispered "Hiya, Champ," and the two champions hugged—and wept.

AUGUST 1966
PRICE 75c

THE MAGAZINE FOR MEN

In Defense of Cassius Clay

By Floyd Patterson

THE GAY WAY TO DODGE THE DRAFT

This in-your-face cover expressed the deep-down knowledge among college students (who were probably *Esquire* magazine's biggest readers and were known to be plastering our covers all over their dorm rooms) that the Vietnam War stunk and that any way to stay out of it was (supposedly) morally acceptable. The model was a Columbia University football player, a very tough hetero. Millions of college students from those days, many of whom became the movers and shakers of our culture, remember *Esquire* magazine and its covers in the '60s with great admiration and respect.

P.S. The great guitarist Jimi Hendrix told editor Harold Hayes that a few years earlier he actually faked being gay – and the army threw him the hell out.

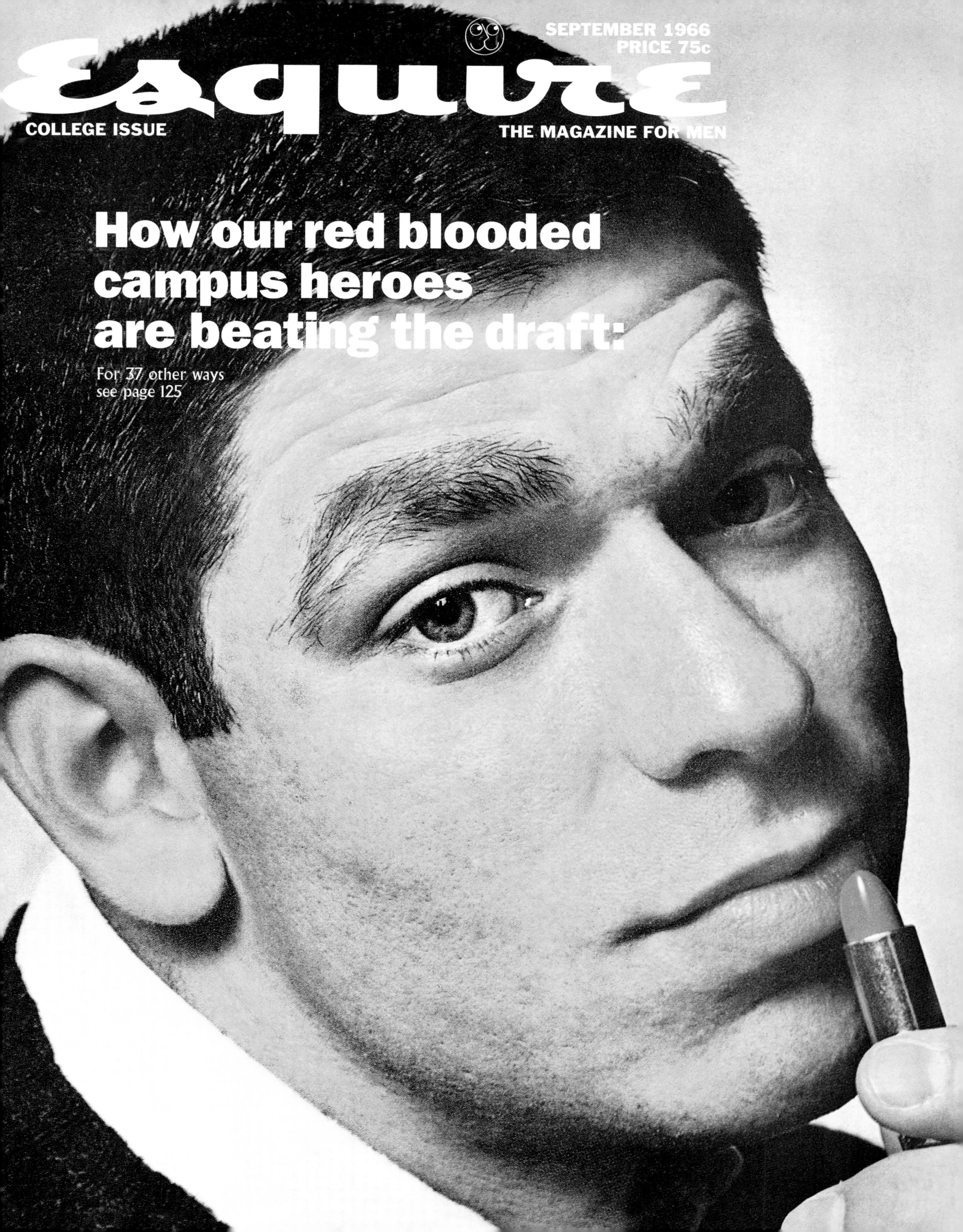
SEPTEMBER 1966
PRICE 75c
Esquire
COLLEGE ISSUE
THE MAGAZINE FOR MEN
How our red blooded
campus heroes
are beating the draft:
For 37 other ways
see page 125

A PREMATURE INDICTMENT OF THE VIETNAM WAR

The words are those of an American soldier in Vietnam, as reported by John Sack in a lengthy article about an infantry company, from basic training through combat. This sentence leaped out at me from Sack's description of a search-and-destroy mission. The words are a G.I.'s horrified reaction as he comes upon the body of a dead Vietnamese child. This cover appeared early in the war, almost two years before the world heard of My Lai (where as many as 500 old men, women, children, and babies were slaughtered by G.I.'s). But in 1966, "only" 350,000 Americans were in Vietnam and "only" 6,000 had died there. The outcry against the war was getting louder, but mostly on the college campuses. As a nation, we were still in a deep sleep, and we never dreamed of My Lai. In fact, the notion that just one American soldier could kill just one Asian child, even inadvertently, was bitter medicine in 1966. The cover screamed to the world that something was wrong, terribly wrong. Good American boys were trapped in an evil war, with no end in sight. *Esquire* was sharply criticized by many readers for this "premature" indictment of the war itself. With mind-numbing hatred of the "gooks" (a racist insult used by most G.I.'s in the Korean and Vietnam wars), the carnage dragged on for years to come, and concern about killing a little child became quaint. (Small potatoes. What the hell, we were killing a little country.) Thirty years later, the secretary of defense war-guru Robert McNamara, whose number-crunching lies and blind obedience to "his president" prolonged and exacerbated this brutally immoral war, disingenuously admitted that "we" had been wrong to fight it. Big Mac's book sales totaled more than the 58,000 American deaths (but considerably fewer than the three million slaughtered Vietnamese).

"Oh my God –we hit a little girl."

The true story of M Company.
From Fort Dix to Vietnam.

THE DUMMY ON LYNDON'S KNEE

When Hubert Humphrey was defending President Lyndon Johnson's Vietnam War escalations, Harold Hayes assigned a writer to do a major piece on the vice president. As the article was being written, I designed this punishing image of HHH as LBJ's dummy (sculpted by the talented Stan Glaubach). Lyndon Johnson was tied up at the time picking out mud huts to bomb in North Vietnam, so I never asked him to pose. The photograph was shot in a studio, using a body-double as large as LBJ. Then I decapitated the photograph and substituted the president's head (one of my notorious transplants in those precomputer days).

When Hayes read the article, he called me to kill the cover. The writer had done a *sympathetic*, pro-Humphrey piece. But when Harold saw my ventriloquist and dummy, he thought the cover was too good to kill. So on the right-hand corner of the foldout, we inserted those three lines that we hoped would do right by Hubert. Two years later, when I was in the veep's office in Washington for a meeting on political advertising, I was astounded to see the cover hanging on the wall of his anteroom. I told Humphrey that I was the author of that masterpiece.

"You no-good sonofabitch," he told me straight out.

"Well, then why do you have it on your wall?"

I asked the vice president. "Because," he said, "maybe it's right."

Esquire

NOVEMBER 1966
PRICE 75c

THE MAGAZINE FOR MEN

"I have known
for 16 years
his courage,
his wisdom,
his tact,
his persuasion,
his judgment, and
his leadership."

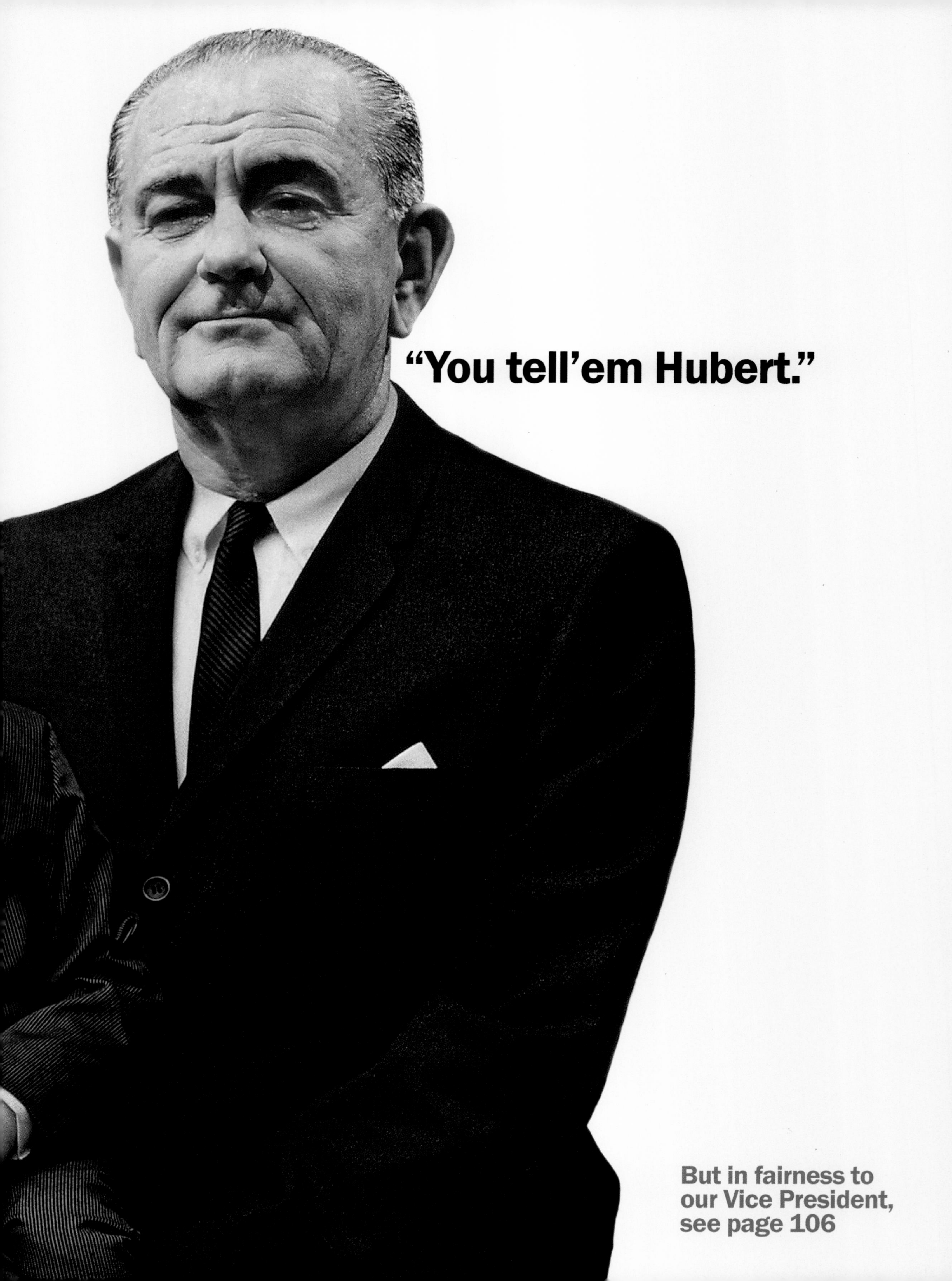
"You tell'em Hubert."
But in fairness to
our Vice President,
see page 106

*HAROLD HAYES
REVVING UP HIS SUPERB
EDITORIAL STAFF, 1966.*

VROOOOM...

I held out almost three years before I gave
Esquire my second cheesecake cover (see page 58).
When this December 1966 issue featured
the classic bikes men loved best, I asked the firebrand
Claudia Cardinale if she would mount
a Triumph for me. She hopped on like a pro,
bellowed away in her lush Italian tongue
on all cylinders, and revved up a lot of engines.
(My only problem was that this first
real "girlie" cover was such a big seller, I knew
Harold Hayes would be pressured for more.)

DECEMBER 1966
PRICE $1
Esquire
THE MAGAZINE FOR MEN
Claudia Cardinale shows you
how to be a good girl *today*.
The New 7 Deadly Sins

"WHAT'S NEW, MR. LOIS, OL' BUDDY?" "I GIVE UP, MR. HAYES. I'M SENDING YOU ANOTHER DAMN GIRLIE COVER."

From the very first cover I created for Harold Hayes in 1962, *Esquire* newsstand sales and circulation grew dramatically. Nonetheless, the magazine's ad-sales gang bitched and moaned, fearful of my "controversial" covers.Though ad pages also rose dramatically through the Hayes decade, some of my provocateur covers scared some agencies into pulling their monthly ads. But in the sexist '60s, the ad bunch was comfortable with "girlie" covers, and they hounded Hayes for Lois cheesecake. *Esquire*'s owners, hoping for a pinup trend after the successful Claudia Cardinale cover I created (see page 98), pushed Hayes for yet another. Though I tell my share of sexist jokes, Hayes knew I didn't intend to harken back to *Esquire*'s "dirty old man" Esky imagery. So that Southern Baptist preacher's son, once again, politely but embarrassingly, asked for tits and ass. (Hell, I'd given them Claudia Cardinale's T & A only two months earlier!) As I remember my reaction, I said, "Harold, ol' pal—you got it!" I knew the great editor was planning an issue on *The New American Woman.* The inspiration for this unchivalrous *Esquire* cover was a sexist and racist joke, popular in those prefeminist days: A young Bronx housewife is hanging laundry on the roof of her apartment house. She slips and falls off the roof, landing headfirst in a garbage pail. A Chinese laundryman walks by, spots her derriere, shapely legs, and womanly charms and says: "Americans very funny people. In China, good for ten years yet." As we all know, Asians venerate age, whereas "The New American Woman is through at 21!" When Hayes slowly and indulgently pulled my belligerent anti-girlie cover from the envelope and saw my stuffed tomato, he ate it up. (But he never asked for a girlie cover again.)

The New American Woman:
through at 21.

TAMEST EVENT ON KIDS TV THAT DAY: RUBY KILLS OSWALD

This May 1967 cover dealt with a decisive TV moment, on November 24, 1963, when Jack Ruby shot Lee Harvey Oswald dead, live, in front of millions, old and young. Four years later, *Esquire* ran a story on Ruby's tortured reasoning for depriving America of the possibility of learning the full truth about the abominable assassination of President Kennedy. Photographer Dick Richards and I showed the moment an all-American kid, mouth agape, mirroring the infamous victim on his black-and-white TV screen, started to grow up with live violence in his carpeted den, complete with an all-American hamburger and a Coke.

MAY 1967
PRICE 75¢

Esquire

THE MAGAZINE FOR MEN

Why Jack Ruby killed Lee Oswald... an untold story.

MY BATTERED BEAUTY

Wouldn't you think a 1967 cover dramatizing violence against women would be applauded by women's groups in America?
Not the National Organization for Women. They busted my balls. (Beats me why.) NOW's pioneering battle for women's rights and against sexism in the late '60s was admirable, but I thought at times misdirected. The issue of battered women was considered taboo and was just not discussed in those days, so my visualization of it on a men's magazine cover was a shocker. Ursula Andress, the stunning beauty of James Bond fame (*Dr. No*, 1962) was courageous enough to pose as the symbol of abuse towards women. Stacked next to the typically bland and inane *Vogue*, *Harper's Bazaar*, and *McCall's* covers, my battered *Esquire* beauty was a knockout.

JULY 1967
PRICE 75¢
Esquire
THE MAGAZINE FOR MEN
Our growing obsession with violence.

CAMPUS WARRIOR

After we won the great war against fascism, the scare of the "red menace"
plunged America into the fearful period of McCarthyism. Shamefully,
we were becoming exactly the kind of society we had fought so valiantly against.
Our "police action" against the North Koreans, which drew in the Chinese,
cost us almost 40,000 dead (20,000 fewer than 'Nam, but in one-third the time).
The American people had been apathetic about the Korean "conflict"
but grew sickened with the loss of life in Vietnam. Fighting a war on foreign shores
to protect against the encroachment of communism didn't mean
a damn to the average American, and young men dodged the draft in droves.
The poor got nailed, and college students were deferred. No other
prominent magazine in America questioned the war, let alone attacked it.
The hawks were flying. But Hayes let me run ten *Esquire* covers
that said the war sucked. Many students loved America and idealized
North Vietnam's role in the war as a utopian experiment
in freedom and self-determination. On college faculties, many scholars
of cultural and political philosophy opposed the war. They watched
television reports of American firepower being used to suppress a peasant
rebellion against oppression that resembled the American Revolution
we were so proud of! I firmly believed all this and knew the "Domino Theory"
was a con job. But in an unexpected flip-flop, this cover snidely took
a shot at the antiwar activists who were raising hell on campuses. I rationalized
it as a parody of the self-righteousness and self-importance
of much of the growing antiwar movement. I depicted "campus warriors"
as long-haired nerds who were just trying to save their asses.
For the life of me, I couldn't figure out what possessed me to do the cover,
until my rabbi, ex-marine lieutenant Harold Hayes, said, "George,
you couldn't help it. You're a pissed-off Korean vet!" To this day, I take heat
for the cover from my wife, Rosie, a fighter against McCarthyism,
a young Korean War wife, and a proto-demonstrator against the Vietnam War.

If you think the war in Vietnam is hell, you ought to see what's happening on campus, baby.

SVETLANA STALIN AND HER FATHER'S MUSTACHE

When Joe Stalin's daughter came to the U.S. in 1967,
her face showed up on the cover of every magazine except
Popular Mechanics. Newsstands from New York to
California were transformed into photo galleries of a motherly
Svetlana Stalin. And she was becoming a bore.
I felt that anyone who told stories about her old man was
a lousy fink, no matter what line of work he was in.
Then *Esquire* planned a lead article on Stalin's little girl, and I was
stuck with the deadly problem of coming up
with another Svetlana cover. Garry Wills' story was at least
a skeptical piece. It described her weirdo
hang-ups with assorted religions. It analyzed how she was
taken in hand by the smart boys in publishing
and our red-baiting State Department when she came
to the United States with her hot manuscript
about life with father Josef. I developed a mental block
against Svetlana, and the cover idea just wouldn't
materialize. I covered my wall with all the previous magazine
covers of her, and they were all alike.
Then it came to me. I grabbed a grease pencil and
scribbled away. Some people were offended
by this cover because Svetlana had been elevated to
sainthood by the time it appeared.
To those people I can only say: your father's mustache.

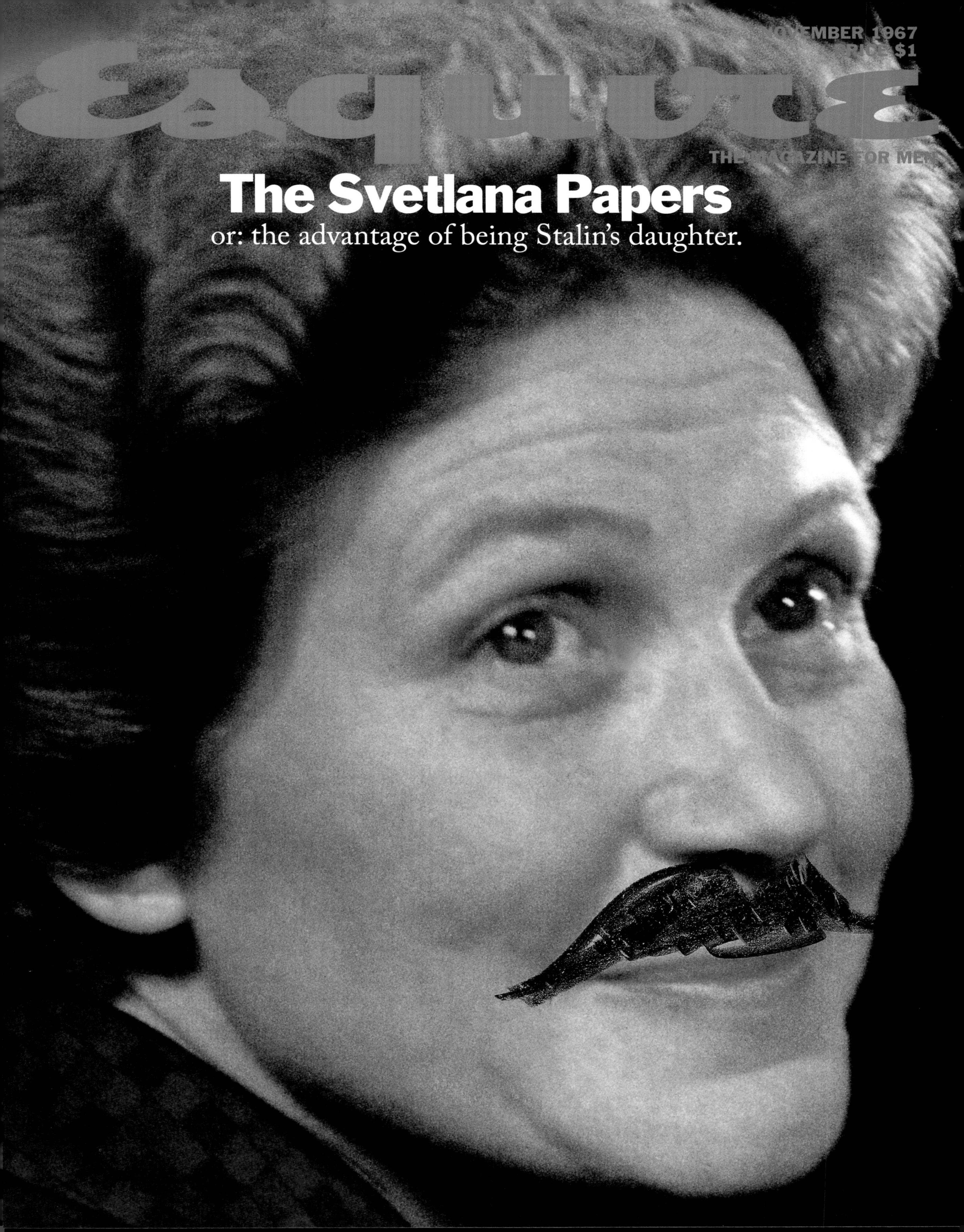
The Svetlana Papers
or: the advantage of being Stalin's daughter.

THE BALL(S) OF TRUMAN CAPOTE

On the night of November 28,1966, Truman Capote threw "a little masked ball" reminiscent of Versailles in 1788, in honor of the *Washington Post* president Katharine Graham, and invited 540 of his closest friends. Rose Kennedy, Frank Sinatra and Mia Farrow, William and Babe Paley, Andy Warhol, Tallulah Bankhead, John Kenneth Galbraith, Harold Prince, and William F. Buckley, Jr., were among those anointed and summoned to the Grand Ballroom of the Plaza Hotel in New York, wearing masks and dressed in black and white. They joined "Betty" Bacall and Jerry Robbins dancing the night away.
Years had gone by without any important writing by Capote. He was a great writer but consumed by hobnobbing with the rich and famous, who treated him like a Pekingese sitting on a needlepoint pillow for them to pet.
An anonymous poem of the time went this way:

Truman Ca-potty
Is not nearly as dotty
As some of the people
Who went to his party.

The complete guest list was, believe it or not, published in *The New York Times*.
A year later, the world was still abuzz about Truman's Ball.
The Gods of Power (celebrity, cultural, and political) spoke of it as Truman's greatest coup. Norman Mailer's deft backstab was, "To me, that party was greater than any of his books!"
So I tried to put all the spin to rest with a final, sour-grapes cover depicting an eclectic and unmasked group sweetly sticking their uninvited tongues out at Capote.

P.S. The only person with the hubris ever to outdo Truman Capote was the flamboyant Malcolm Forbes, with his $2 million airlift shindig in Morocco for 880 pals in 1989. In an ad for No Excuses jeans, I gave him one of my monthly No Excuses Awards:
"To Malcolm Forbes. For feeding 880 hungry people in Africa."
They don't give parties like that anymore.
Of course not. They're all dead.

The Party Poopers
(clockwise from upper left):
NFL great Jim Brown
Screen star Kim Novak
Leading man Tony Curtis
California governor Edmund "Pat" Brown
TV showman Ed Sullivan
Baseball legend Casey Stengel
"Georgy Girl" Lynn Redgrave
JFK press secretary Pierre Salinger

"We wouldn't have come even if you *had* invited us, Truman Capote!"

THE ANGEL COHN

To illustrate a self-serving piece by Roy Cohn in which he rationalized his skulduggery as the demagogue senator Joe McCarthy's favorite gofer during the '50s, I asked him to pose as the angel he thought he was. I made no bones about the photo: He was to be shown wearing a halo that was visibly pinned on, a self-applied halo. He posed for the shot and said as he was leaving the studio, "I suppose you're going to pick the ugliest one." "You bet," I said. "I hate your guts." For once in his life he was speechless. (In the 2003 television miniseries of Tony Kushner's award-winning play *Angels in America*, for a scene that takes place in Roy Cohn's office, director Mike Nichols had my cover recreated, replacing Cohn with the actor Al Pacino, framed and hanging on the wall. It would seem that the real Roy Cohn thought my cover did him justice.)

P.S. Upon seeing this image of Cohn on the February 1968 cover of *Esquire*, Senator Robert Kennedy told me, "That's the closest Roy Cohn will ever get to heaven."

FEBRUARY 1968
PRICE $1
Esquire
THE MAGAZINE FOR MEN
Joe McCarthy's Roy Cohn
tells it like it was.

SHOWING MUHAMMAD ALI AS A MARTYR FOR REFUSING TO FIGHT IN A BAD WAR

In 1967, Muhammad Ali, the world's heavyweight champion, refused induction into the U.S. Army. He had converted to the Nation of Islam, and under the tutelage of Elijah Muhammad, he became a Black Muslim minister. When Ali refused military service as a conscientious objector because of his new religion, a federal jury sentenced him to five years in jail for draft evasion. Boxing commissions then stripped him of his title and denied him the right to fight. Ali was in the prime of his fighting years but wasn't allowed in a ring. He was widely condemned as a draft-dodger and even a traitor. When Cassius Clay had became a Muslim, he had also become a martyr. In 1968, while he was waiting for his appeal to reach the U.S. Supreme Court, I wanted to pose him as Saint Sebastian, modeled after the 15th-century painting by Francesco Botticini that hangs in the Metropolitan Museum of Art. I contacted Ali and explained my concept, and he flew posthaste to New York to pose. At the studio, I showed him a postcard of the painting to illustrate the stance. He studied it with enormous concentration. Suddenly he blurted out, "Hey, George, this cat's a Christian!" I blurted back, "Holy Moses, you're right, Champ!" I explained to Ali that Saint Sebastian was a Roman soldier who survived execution by arrows after converting to Christianity. He was then clubbed to death and has gone down in history as the definitive martyr. Before we could affix any arrows to Ali, he got on the phone with his religious leader, Elijah Muhammad. Ali explained the painting in excruciating detail. He was concerned about the propriety of using a Christian source for the portrayal of his martyrdom. He finally put me, a nonpracticing Greek Orthodox, on the phone. After a lengthy theological discussion, Elijah gave me his OK. I exhaled, and we shot this portrait of a deified man against the authorities. When I saw the first transparency, I believe my exact words to the photographer were, "Jesus Christ, it's a masterpiece." *Esquire* had a sensational cover, and it was reproduced and sold as a protest poster and hung in college dorms all over America. Three years later, the U.S. Supreme Court unanimously threw out Ali's conviction. Allah be praised!

P.S. In a review of the MoMA exhibit in celebration of the induction of the *Esquire* covers into its permanent collections, the Associated Press wrote: "the most iconic image of the '60s was Ali as Saint Sebastian, tying together the incendiary issues of the Vietnam War, race, and religion. The image is so powerful that some people remember where they were when they saw it for the first time."

APRIL 1968
PRICE $1

Esquire

THE MAGAZINE FOR MEN

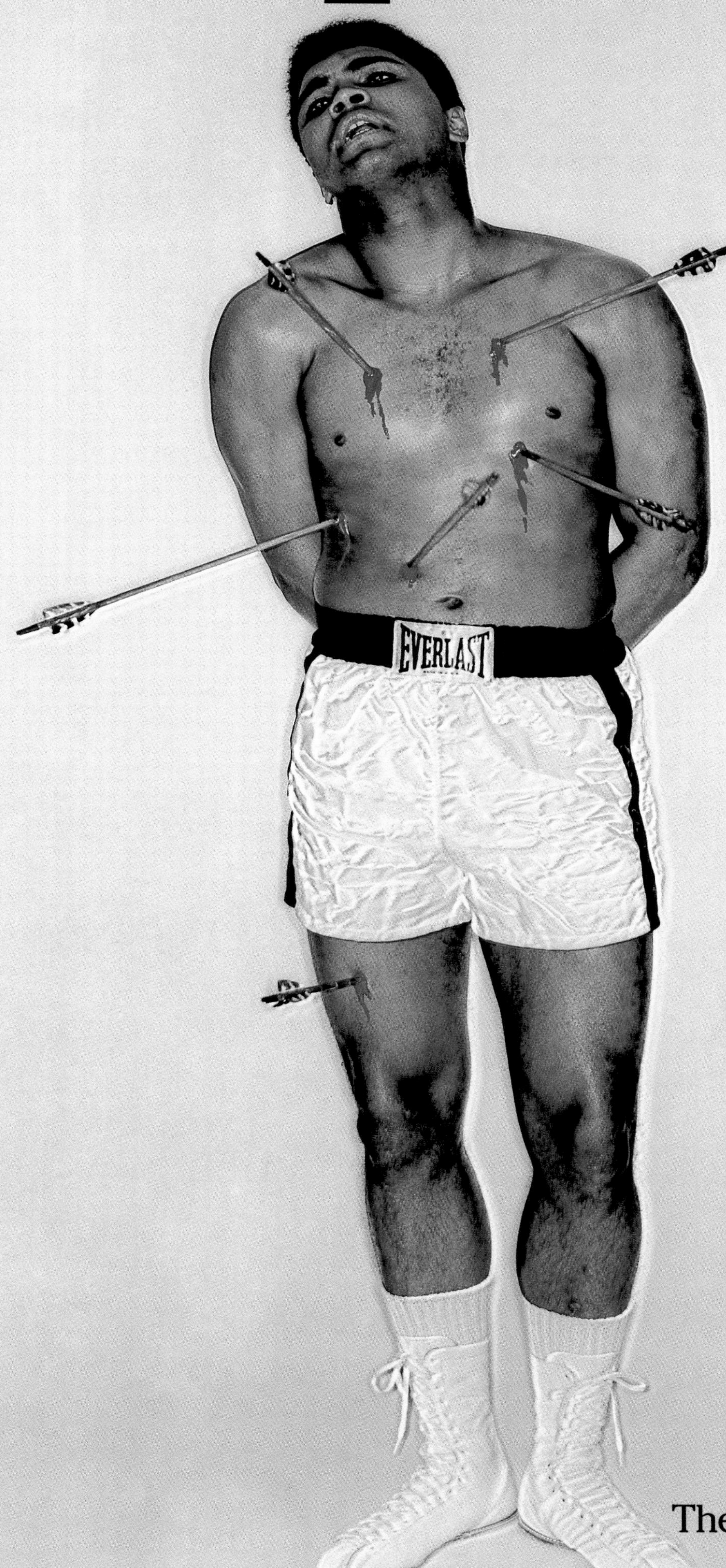

The Passion of Muhammad Ali

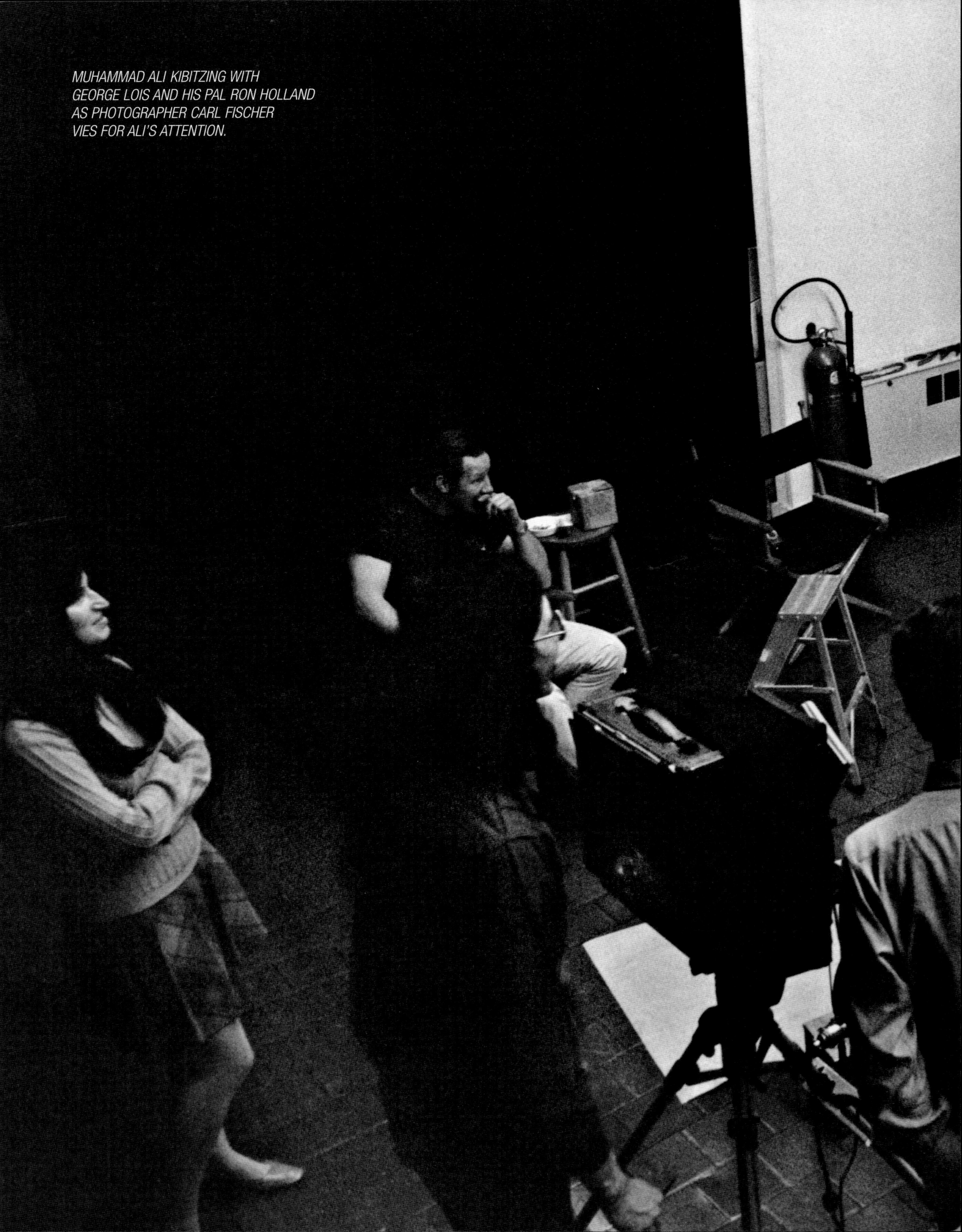

MUHAMMAD ALI KIBITZING WITH GEORGE LOIS AND HIS PAL RON HOLLAND AS PHOTOGRAPHER CARL FISCHER VIES FOR ALI'S ATTENTION.

EVERLAST

HOW I TAUGHT NIXON TO USE MAKEUP AND BECOME PRESIDENT

I did this cover in the spring of 1968, before Richard Nixon was nominated, while he was still hustling around the country begging for delegates. This composite shot was a satirical comment on the 1960 TV debates, when the Whittier whiz with the 5 o'clock shadow lost to John F. Kennedy because he looked evil in front of the cameras. (Nixon acknowledged he had lost because of the "perspiration over my upper lip.") I located this profile shot in the wire-service archives and had four hands photographed, including the one wielding the lipstick. What's interesting about this image is the way Nixon's gang reacted to it. Shortly after it appeared, editor Harold Hayes got a phone call from Nixon's press secretary, Ron Ziegler. He was miffed. In fact, he was incensed. You know why? The lipstick. He said it was an attack on Nixon's masculinity. Those birds in Tricky Dick's corner didn't laugh too easily. He called Hayes a "lousy liberal" and hung up. The Watergate tapes later revealed the astounding paranoia that consumed Nixon and his clean-cut goons, many of whom went to jail. Ziegler dismissed the first report of the break-in at the Watergate Hotel as a "third-rate burglary," but within two years, President Nixon resigned under the threat of impeachment for his involvement in the break-in and cover-up. After his campaign promise to end the Vietnam War, Nixon had exceeded all our fears when he mercilessly prolonged the slaughter for almost six bloody years, as he pilloried Vietnam War resisters and prompted and engaged in the horror of the Watergate scandal, forever staining the office of the presidency.

P.S. The subsequent creepy triumph of Richard Nixon at the Republican National Convention, and the shock of his conspiratorial presidency added to our nation's unbearable stress, driven by the war in Vietnam and the revolution in civil rights; it all resulted in a loony psychological meltdown in America that continues to this day. My only regret as a cultural provocateur was that I wasn't allowed to continue portraying the incongruous mélange of American history on the covers of *Esquire* past the '60s, all the way through the notorious Nixon, the Ford that ran without a full tank, the Reagan ramblings, the catatonic Carter years, the Bush lip-readings, the Clinton capers, and last but certainly not least, the Bush-Cheney catastrophes.

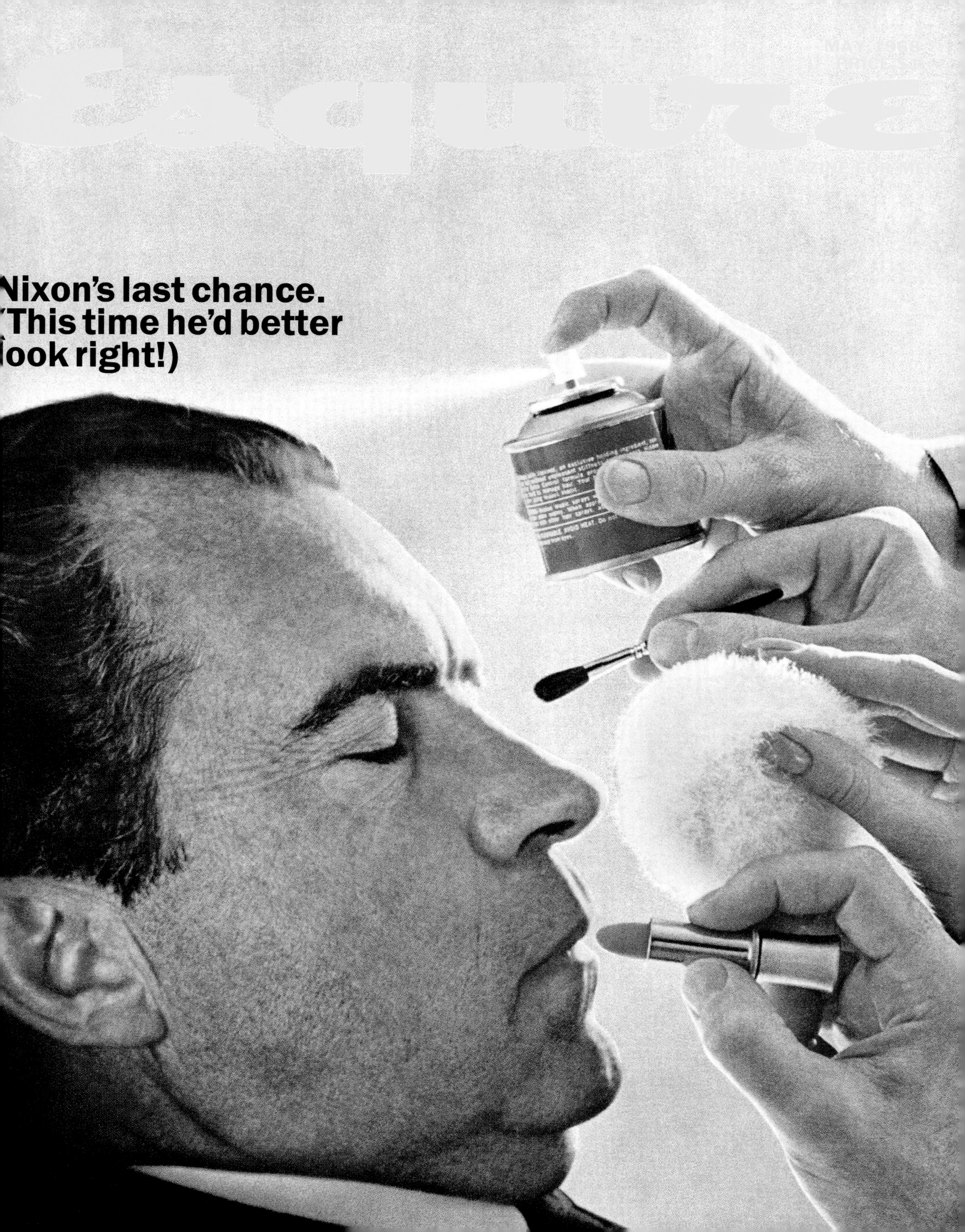
MAY 1968
PRICE $1
Esquire
THE MAGAZINE FOR MEN
Nixon's last chance.
(This time he'd better
look right!)

TROUBLE ON ICE (AND THE MAYOR OF NEW YORK COPS OUT)

In 1968, America once again anticipated a hot, troubled summer in that steamy time of racial conflict and "civil disorders." The "white devil" diatribes of Malcolm X and the fearsome threats of Huey Newton, Eldridge Cleaver, and their Black Panthers made clear to the white world that the black man, up to no good, had retribution in his heart. And it was abundantly clear to the black man that the racist society he grew up in would never blossom into Lyndon Johnson's proposed Great Society. The black man in America had no future. So when the summer came, both jobless fathers and their neglected sons were in the streets, fuming, fussing, and firing. Ralph Ellison had previously written about the "invisible man" of the '50s, but now that black man had become all too visible, mugging in the alleys and rioting in the streets. White America, in its secret and bitter heart, wanted black America to just go away. Isolation, assimilation, expulsion, destruction: Any means would do. Back in 1963, with John F. Kennedy in the Oval Office and Americans congratulating themselves on having done something about race relations, James Baldwin published *The Fire Next Time*, foreseeing the rioting in the mid-'60s in Watts, Newark, Detroit, Washington, Chicago, and other American cities. *Esquire* interviewed this powerful and prophetic spokesman of the "Negro" two days after the funeral of Dr. Martin Luther King, Jr., during a countrywide nightmare of riots and martial law. Baldwin's biting, embittered, and fatalistic attack on the white establishment appalled the readers of *Esquire*. And my searing visual image of real life, ass-kicking young black men, attempting to cool off in an actual Harlem icehouse, added to the heat. It infuriated both African-American leaders and white neighborhoods that feared an all-out black revolution. It also scared the hell out of New York mayor John Lindsay. The handsome, patrician WASP, who was elected mayor in 1965 as a white knight of urban politics, was a no-show after he had promised me that he would pose in the shadows of the icehouse along with his seven young constituents. Waiting in the eerie silence of the strangely beautiful ice-filled room, one of the brooding young men finally chuckled: "You didn't really think that blond, blue-eyed motherfucker had the balls to show up in our 'hood, did you, Georgie-boy?"

JULY 1968
PRICE $1
Esquire
THE MAGAZINE FOR MEN
James Baldwin
tells us all
how to cool it
this summer.

YO!

The year 1968 had turned ugly beyond belief, with the sound of the world ending: the proliferation of the Vietnam War with a murderous Tet offensive; the murder of Dr. Martin Luther King, Jr.; out-of-control city riots resulting from King's assassination; the killing of our probable next president, Robert Kennedy; all culminating in the riots and police brutality during the Democratic National Convention. For the August issue of *Esquire*, Harold Hayes planned to run a piece on a radical effort taking place to organize a union (!) in the American military. The very thought that the U.S. Army could be unionized, midwar, in the midst of the apocalyptic year of 1968, surely warranted some attention from me on an *Esquire* cover. And that's why this ethnic G.I., recently drafted, chewing out a Waspy four-star general, commanded a lot of attention. In fear that this cover would cause a G.I. revolt (huh?), the issue was banned at U.S. military bases throughout the world.

P.S. I never considered the scenario on my cover as totally far-fetched. In 1952, I had been drafted and was taking basic training at Camp Gordon, Georgia, deep in the Jim Crow south. My company commander, upon hearing me respond to a morning roll call with my Noo Yawk "Yo!" strode up to me and bellowed, "Another Noo Yawk-Jew-fag-niggah-lova." I respectfully whispered a Bronx-accented, "Go fuck yourself, sir," did eight weeks' "company punishment," and soon found myself in Korea.

AUGUST 1968
PRICE $1

Esquire

THE MAGAZINE FOR MEN

Exclusive!
The Plot to Unionize the U.S. Army

"HAIR, HAIR, HAIR, FLOW IT, SHOW IT, LONG AS GOD CAN GROW IT"

Most Americans over 30 years old hated
hippies (translation: any kid with too much hair),
so I rubbed it in their faces when
I showed long-haired Tiny Tim (*Tiptoe Through the Tulips*),
long-haired Michael Pollard (*Bonnie and Clyde*),
and long-haired Arlo Guthrie (*Alice's Restaurant*)
as three of the Beautiful People and
favorite performers of seven million college kids
in 1968. Boy, this cover pissed off
America, but the youth of America ate it up.
(In the almost six years that I had been
working with Harold Hayes, there was general
acknowledgement in the culture that my
Esquire covers were defining the times we lived in.
But this depiction of the campus heroes of the
day defined the *hairstyles* of the times we lived in.)

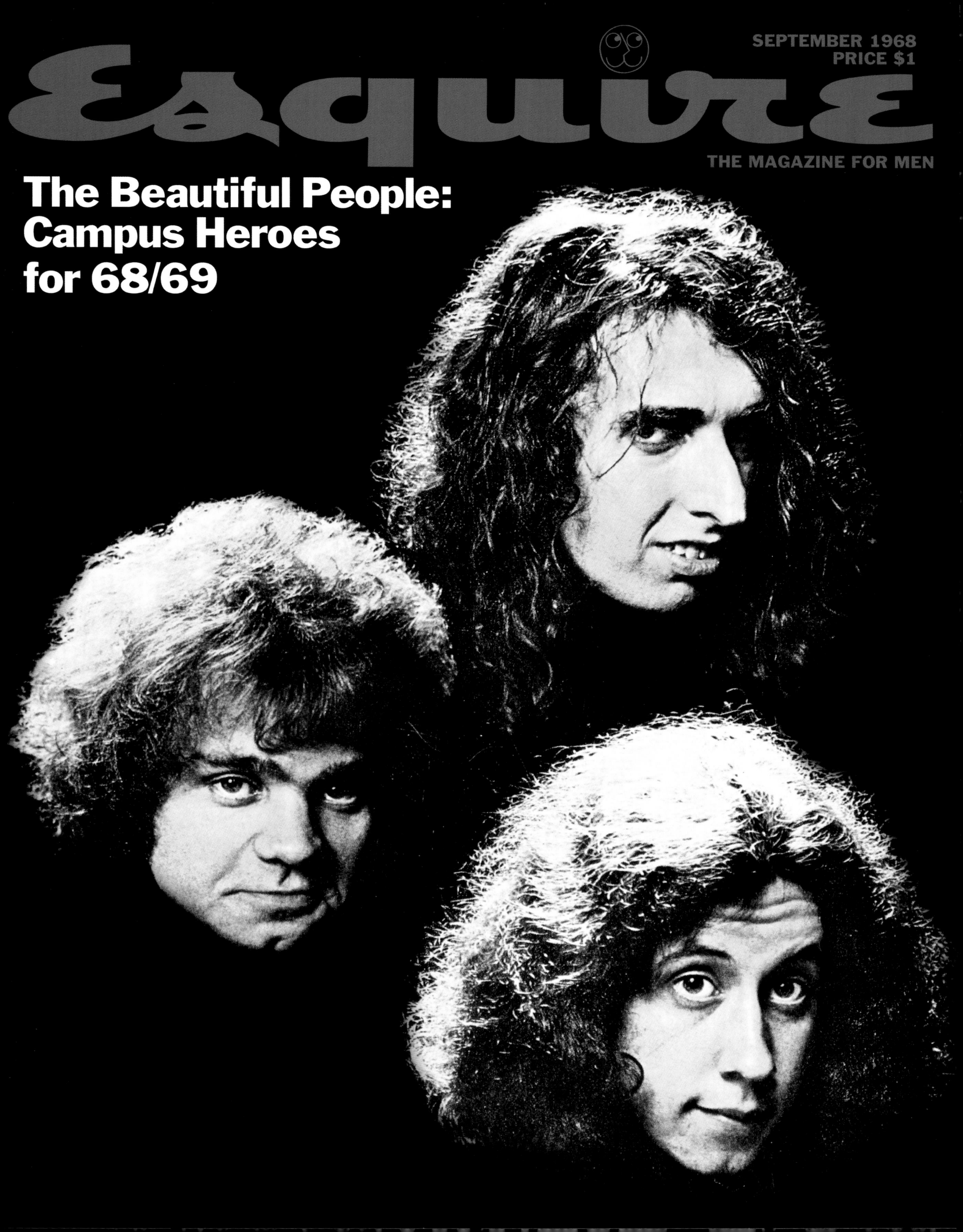
SEPTEMBER 1968
PRICE $1
Esquire
THE MAGAZINE FOR MEN
The Beautiful People:
Campus Heroes
for 68/69

APOTHEOSIS!

The '60s had been a decade of titanic crusades, as protests and marches advanced the fight for civil rights and women's liberation, even as the Vietnam War and its atrocities escalated. The war had laid a curse on America, like the curse that William Faulkner said slavery had previously laid on our nation. The insanity culminated in the horrific year of 1968, when Dr. Martin Luther King, Jr. and Robert Kennedy were both assassinated in a span of nine weeks. I plead guilty to shockingly irreverent concepts for many covers. But in 1968, the times pleaded for equally shocking reverence. On the cover of *Esquire*'s definitive 35th anniversary issue, I showed our assassinated leaders, the three most mourned Americans since FDR, hauntingly watching over Arlington National Cemetery. In this hagiographic fantasy, we pay homage to an idealized, saintlike John F. Kennedy, Robert Kennedy, and Dr. King, in a dreamlike epitaph on the murder of American goodness, and a prayer for the resurrection of American ideals.

35th Anniversary Issue of

Esquire

Salvaging the 20th Century

OCTOBER 1968

$1.50

THE 1968 DEMOCRATIC CONVENTION: "THE WHOLE WORLD IS WATCHING"

Only Harold Hayes had the guts and the nuts to assemble this
stunning team of underground intellectual mavericks
to go to the fateful Democratic National Convention in Chicago in 1968
and report to the nation. A debilitated and despondent
LBJ had shocked the nation by quitting, lobbing his Vietnam
hot potato to a succeeding president. The television
coverage of bitter wrangling in the arena, intercut with Chicago cops
lobbing tear gas and splitting open young demonstrators'
heads as they chanted "The whole world is watching," laced together
by film footage of G.I.'s in mortal combat in Vietnam,
traumatized the nation. Originally, Carl Fischer had been sent to
Chicago to simply shoot the unholy quartet at the convention.
But watching the Chicago carnage, I came up with my cover idea
of a Christlike image of a jeans-clad student, lying in a
bloody gutter at the feet of the wildest literary men of the time:
Jean Genet (the French high priest of decadence),
William Burroughs (the expatriate Beat Generation spokesman),
Terry Southern (the irreverent *Candy* man),
and John Sack (the antiwar war correspondent).
I called Carl and described the shot. When he tried to stage it in Chicago,
he damn-near got himself and *Esquire*'s reporting team arrested.
So I told them to hightail it back to New York, and we grabbed this dramatic
image in the "safe" streets of Harlem. (The convention
went on to nominate the shell of Hubert Humphrey, who had shrunk
to being a yes-man to his president. HHH fell victim to the
bitterness of the fray, ran an inept campaign, and got beat by Tricky Dick's
"secret plan" that promised to bring our boys home by Christmas.
After 27,000 *more* dead G.I.'s, home they came.)

NOVEMBER 1968
PRICE $1
Esquire
THE MAGAZINE FOR MEN
PRESS 1968
PRESS 1968
Jean Genet,
William Burroughs,
Terry Southern,
John Sack,
–Chicago!

DREAM GIRL OR AX MURDERESS?

This cover dealt with a macho piece in *Esquire* on fantasy women,
written almost instinctively as a defense
against the budding feminist war on the atmosphere
of sexism that had been a way of life in America.
In retrospect, through the Hayes years, *Esquire* had championed
the intelligent and accomplished woman.
But, while eschewing the '30s, '40s, and '50s dirty-old-man
Esky tradition of depicting women as sex objects,
Hayes and his gang of bawdy editors pricked a lot of
sexual balloons with loads of lusty laughs.
I rose to the occasion by tackling the traditional dichotomy
of a man's fantasy of women: that of the desire
for the woman who could play the parts of both the Madonna
and the whore to satisfy his body and soul.
The young supermodel Lauren Hutton and I dreamt up
a quartet of sexual types and melded them
into one desirable woman. That she wound up looking nuts,
or possibly like an avenging feminist ax murderess,
added to its accuracy. Oddly, this cover was a precursor
of a legendary First Lady who could shed skins
faster than a snake. In one decade, she went from a shy
little-girl-lost (Jacqueline Bouvier), to a merry,
caring mommy and most glamorous First Lady (Jackie Kennedy),
to a bereaved saint (Mrs. Kennedy), to a
fortune-seeker, dragging her children into a decadent world of
gaudy appetites (Jackie Onassis) culminating in her
final role of Great Goddess, a combination of all women (Jackie KO!).

DECEMBER 1968
PRICE $1
Esquire
Season's Greetings! 4 naughty dreams to last you till March.
Dream 1: the Sadist
Dream 2: the Virgin
Dream 3: the Babysitter
Dream 4: the French Maid

THE VERY FIRST HOWARD HUGHES HOAX

This issue sold like hotcakes because at long last the "invisible" Howard Hughes was finally "discovered," which proves once more that you can fool all of the people all of the time. I was simply trying to spoof the idiotic interest in America's best-known, least-seen mystery man. The guy in the white bathrobe is an actor playing Howard Hughes. The woman in the bathing suit is an actress who looked like Hughes' wife, Jean Peters. And the lug playing a bodyguard came from central casting. (Photographer Tasso Vendikos played the paparazzo so well he was detained by the Miami cops.) Everyone thought it was the real thing when this issue came out, but *Time* magazine reported that it was all an elaborate put-on. (Duh!) The press pounced on editor Harold Hayes for an explanation, and he summed up the silly hoo-ha over the mystery celebrity: "What we're doing is an attempt to satirize the whole obsession with the idea that the world is constantly pursuing Mr. Hughes."

P.S. I wonder if Clifford Irving saw this cover back in 1969, three years before he wrote his bogus "authorized" Hughes biography–an incredible paper caper that landed him in the cooler.

Esquire
MARCH 1969
PRICE $1
THE MAGAZINE FOR MEN

Howard Hughes: We see you!

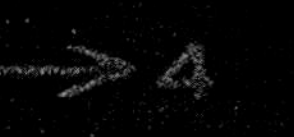

We see you!

See page 73

"AN ESQUIRE COVER OF ME DROWNING IN A CAN OF CAMPBELL'S SOUP? I LOVE IT! BUT GEORGE, AREN'T YOU GONNA HAVE TO BUILD A GIANT CAN OF SOUP?"

ANDY WARHOL

Many of the *Esquire* covers I created in the '60s were planned as montages of photographic elements. In this case, the flamboyant Pop artist Andy Warhol sinking into a Campbell's soup can, printed on the same surface and retouched for perfect realism, was a handmade precursor of the digital assemblage and computer retouching commonly known as Photoshopping, widely used today by every Tom, Dick and Harriet yearning to be a graphic designer. Other photomontage *Esquire* covers, all executed with patience and tender loving care decades before the digital age, were:

The Face of a Hero (page 76),
Sir Lancelot He's Not (page 80),
The Dummy on Lyndon's Knee (page 94),
Tamest Event on Kids TV That Day: Ruby Kills Oswald (page 102),
Svetlana Stalin and Her Father's Mustache (page 108),
How I Taught Nixon to Use Makeup and Become President (page 118),
Apotheosis! (page 126),
Little Big Man (page 150),
The Loews St. Patrick's Marquee (page 152),
Jackie Oh! (page 156),
The Incredible Shrinking Magazine (page 160),
A Cool Dude Superstar Modeling Clothes (page 170).

In today's digital age, the once time-consuming synthesis of the two images would be duck soup.

THREE OF THE DOZENS OF PHOTOS OF ANDY WARHOL GIVING HIS BEST IMITATION OF A DROWNING MAN. *TURN THE PAGE TO SEE ANDY IN THE SOUP...*

ANDY WARHOL BEING DEVOURED BY FAME

This cover has become a symbol of *Esquire*'s juxtaposition of the celebration of pop culture... with the deconstruction of celebrity. The Pop Art movement in America was launched in 1962, with one-man shows by Roy Lichtenstein, James Rosenquist, Tom Wesselmann, Robert Indiana, and Andy Warhol, who became the best known Pop artist of his time, and inexplicably, one of the most famous artists in history. The pervading symbol of the Pop Art movement of that era was Warhol's Campbell's soup can. I've never been able to regard Pop Art as a serious movement. It was the Dada of our time (but not as talented as its father). It used billboards, packages, brand symbols, comic strips, typefaces and you-name-it to make its "statements." I've always thought of Andy as a bold innovator and a smart thinker, but he was a far cry from a Marcel Duchamp or a Man Ray. There's no question, however, that Warhol was a major-league showman. Any guy who can parlay a soup can (not to mention the mundane Brillo box) into personal superstardom may not fit my definition of an artist, but he's certainly hot stuff. When this article in *Esquire* came up, I decided to show him drowning in his own soup. He knew it was a friendly spoof of his original claim to fame, but he still enjoyed that fame enough to welcome his puss on one of those *Esquire* covers. We photographed Warhol and the open can of soup separately (see previous page). When we put Andy into the soup, we almost lost him. (The Bewigged One begged me for years to trade the original art of my cover for one of his Campbell's soup can paintings—worth multimillions today—but I told Andy I would donate the original art to MoMA one day—and in 2008, I did.)

The final decline and total collapse of the American avant-garde.

DOWN WITH RUSSIA—AND UP TO THE MOON!

In one metallic phrase, Winston Churchill slammed down his "Iron Curtain," separating East from West for a half-century of Cold War. Dwight D. Eisenhower continued Harry S. Truman's economic buildup against yesterday's deadly enemies, expending endless effort to outdo and outscrew our feared adversary, the scheming Soviet Union. Constantly raising the ante, both sides squirreled away enough H-bombs to waste the world a hundred times over. The Russians hurled a Sputnik satellite into space, followed by the shocking launch of their first cosmonaut, Yuri Gagarin, becoming the first human in space. Their dizzying success made our heads spin. An abashed JFK decided that the way to reclaimed glory was to aim for the stars. We had to beat the USSR to the future, and the future was space. Multibillions were pumped into the space race, manic and conspicuous consumption to beat out the Russkies. A lunar landing by a manned Apollo 11 would symbolize capitalism's triumph over godless communism, by God. But what American would rocket to fame, and what words should he utter as he became the first human to step into the dust of another world? *Esquire*'s July 1969 issue reported on (and fueled) the national dialogue. But none of the vaunted literary, political, and celebrity minds came close to Neil Armstrong's lofty message on July 20,1969, which traveled farther than any words in history:
"That's one small step for man; one giant leap for mankind."
America got its rocks off.

JULY 1969
PRICE $1

Esquire

THE MAGAZINE FOR MEN

We asked Marshall McLuhan, W.H. Auden, Marianne Moore, R. Buckminster Fuller, Robert Graves, Ayn Rand, Bob Hope, Hubert Humphrey, Tiny Tim, Vladimir Nabokov, Muhammad Ali, John Kenneth Galbraith, Truman Capote, and U Thant:

What words should the first man on the moon utter that will ring through the ages?

UEL FINLEY MORSE

"What hath God wrought."

ALEXANDER GRAHAM BELL

"Watson, come here– I need you."

HENRY MORTON STANLEY

"Dr. Livingstone, I presume?"

CHARLES LINDBERGH

"Well, I made it."

NEIL ARMSTRONG

"Er...ah...well, let's see now."

THE SHOCK OF THE NUDE

After decades of being fed a bland diet of God, family, country,
and the virtues of virginity (when "nice girls" didn't),
our popular culture began to reflect a changing sexual and moral ethos.
Popular entertainment—including the hair-raising
nudity of *Hair*, the deep-throat depiction of homosexuality
in *Midnight Cowboy*, Brando's buttery probing in
Last Tango In Paris, along with the safety of the pill and a budding
drug culture—nonplussed the "decent" people of America.
To dramatize that surprise, I called for the services of the sexiest
stripper in showbiz, Angel Ray of L.A.'s Body Shop fame.
To see a morally shocked stripper watching a flick
of the day seemed to me not only funny but also wittily far-fetched.
The night before we photographed her, after flying
in from California, Angel had, unbeknownst to me, gone to the theater
to see *Oh! Calcutta!* (a famous revue that debuted
Off-Broadway in 1969 with salacious scenes of total nudity,
both male and female). "How did you like it, Angel?"
I innocently asked. Almost blushing, she answered,
"Geez, George... I was so *embarrassed!*" Life imitates art.

Public decency on the screen, stage, and in the streets. The stripper gives her views.

THE KIDS AT WOODSTOCK LOVED THIS COVER...

...but you shoulda heard the cops squeal!
This September 1969 issue of *Esquire* was already on the newsstands, and in the sweaty hands of many who went to Woodstock on August 15, 1969. The many thousands who attended the muddy majesty of the three-day culture-bending event had grown up and matured through the apocalypse of the 60s, affected and sensitive to the seismic changes that continued to unfold around them in those horrific, roller-coaster years:
America's longest and wrongest war (until Iraq),
America's four assassinations,
America's volatile politics,
America's women's movement,
America's black revolution,
America's most putrid presidency (until Bush),
America's obsession with sex, youth, dope, and doom.
Throughout those nasty years, when antiwar demonstrations were met by derision, spit, and street violence, the youth of America vented their disrespect on the mean-spirited arm of the authorities, the police. *Esquire* was barraged with bagfuls of hate mail from cops, but this cover became a favorite of the college crowd and hung in dorms for years.

Back to College Issue

SEPTEMBER 1969
PRICE $1

Esquire

THE MAGAZINE FOR MEN

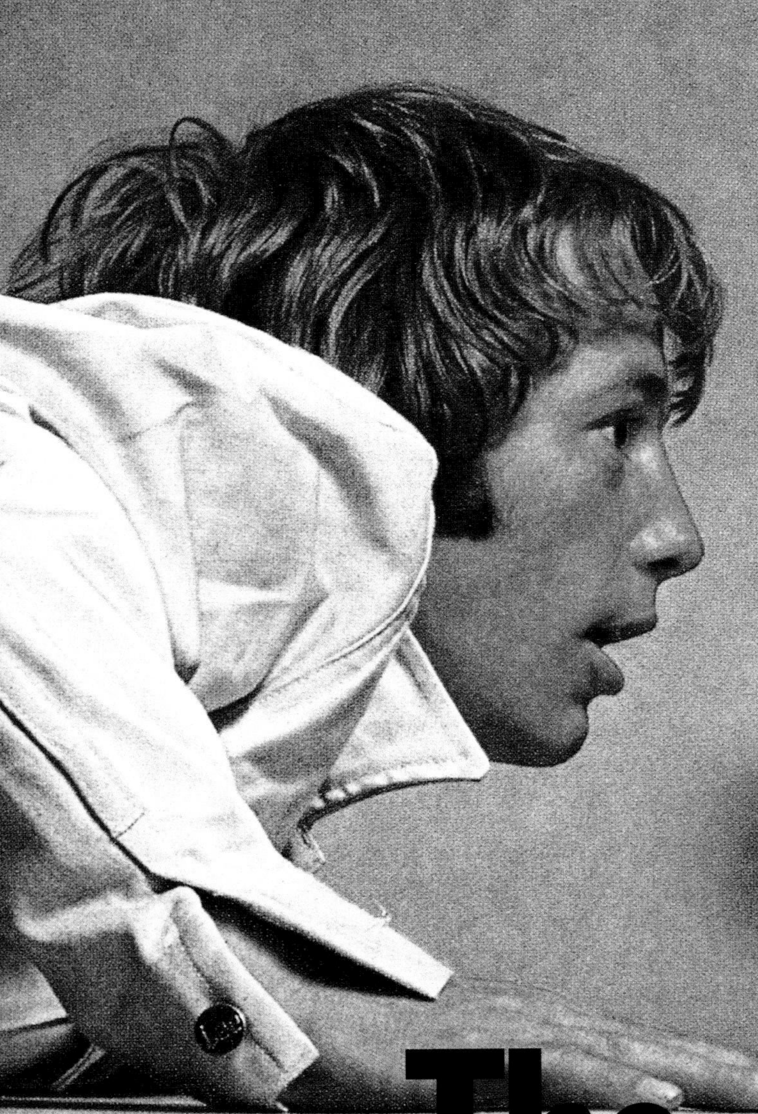

The Kids VS The Pigs

Freshman Orientation Package

12 ANGRY MEN AND A NO-SHOW

In November 1969 I did my third Ali cover (see pages 88 and 114). At the time, the great heavyweight champion remained stripped of his title for refusing military service. We enlisted twelve good souls to climb into the boxing ring (constructed in photographer Ira Mazer's studio to ensure privacy) and publicly support Ali's right to go back to work. One giant who had agreed to join the protest was his fellow Muslim Kareem Abdul-Jabbar of the L.A. Lakers. I envisioned the seven-footer standing tall surrounded by the literary great Truman Capote, the Pop artist Roy Lichtenstein, the sports announcer Howard Cosell, the *12 Angry Men* director Sidney Lumet, the anti-Vietnam War senator Ernest Gruening, and seven others. My dozen heroic combatants patiently waited for more than two hours, but Jabbar, alas, was a no-show. (His explanation to me for his embarrassing absence was that he feared "retaliation," not by the white establishment, but by competing factions in his Muslim world.) Finally, in 1971, the U.S. Supreme Court stood in Ali's corner, and Muhammad went back to work.

NOVEMBER 1969
PRICE $1

THE MAGAZINE FOR MEN

We believe this:

Muhammad Ali deserves the right to defend his title.

1 Richard Benjamin
2 Theodore Bikel
3 Truman Capote
4 Howard Cosell
5 Ernest Gruening
6 Michael Harrington
7 James Earl Jones
8 Roy Lichtenstein
9 Sidney Lumet
10 George Plimpton
11 Budd Schulberg
12 José Torres

And inside,
90 others.

GEORGE LOIS' OFFICE AT
LOIS HOLLAND CALLAWAY, 1969.

WHEN LOIS WASN'T AT HIS AD AGENCY CREATING AD CAMPAIGNS AND ESQUIRE COVERS, HE COULD BE FOUND PLAYING FULL-COURT BASKETBALL AT THE 23RD STREET YMCA OR SITTING COURTSIDE AT KNICKS GAMES IN MADISON SQUARE GARDEN (SHOWN HERE BETWEEN HIS PAL STEVE BERKENFELD AND HIS SONS, LUKE AND HARRY JOE, 1971).

LITTLE BIG MAN

Grab any magazine and cover its logo. They all look the same (and these days, smell the same). That's because every journalism "expert" preaches that if you choose the latest hot star, and your lucky stars are in alignment, that issue will be a best seller. I refused to produce a celebrity cover, as such. To me, that would have been the kiss of death to the "outside-inside" transformation editor Hayes and I had accomplished for *Esquire*. (The magazine had exploded in circulation as Hayes molded it to reflect the attitudes, aspirations, and adrenaline of the American male.) To this day, nine out of ten magazines choose celebrities for their covers, and nine out of ten are wrong. (Oh, I had my fun with famous people but always for a purpose—Ed Sullivan in a Beatles wig, Warhol drowning in his own soup, Svetlana with her father's mustache, Muhammad Ali agonizing as Saint Sebastian.) Nevertheless, eight years into my *Esquire* covers, Hayes had a request. He had just seen a rough cut of Arthur Penn's *Little Big Man* and begged me to slap Dustin Hoffman's mug on the cover. Hoffman, one of America's foremost actors, had a notorious rep with producers and directors for refusing to promote his films. But *Esquire* covers were hot, so he agreed to pose. The young superstar had adopted New York as his home, so I adapted the *Little Big Man* theme for the cover. I showed the diminutive Hoffman standing tall, eyeball-to-eyeball with the Chrysler Building. Twenty years later, I found myself having breakfast with Hoffman and Steve Ross, then the chairman of Time Warner, during the period when my ad campaign "Make time for *Time*" was a hit in the media world. Gobbling up my cereal (and feeling my oats), I proudly preened to Hoffman, who, in 1967, as a struggling Off-Broadway actor, had become an instant star in *The Graduate*: "Remember me? I'm the guy who did that *Esquire* cover of you in 1970." Dusty replied, "*Esquire* cover? I was never on an *Esquire* cover!" Ouch.

JULY 1970
PRICE $1
Esquire
THE MAGAZINE FOR MEN
Dustin Hoffman
grows up!

THE LOEWS ST. PATRICK'S MARQUEE

A good magazine cover, like a strong package design,
usually explains what's inside. A good issue of
Esquire enabled me to make a personal comment
about what I thought the magazine was trying
to say. And this wildly inventive, deadly serious publication
was magazine journalism at its peak of achievement.
The August 1970 issue featured a sheaf of articles on the spreading
youth culture, but it seemed to lack a definitive
point of view. So I gave it one. In my mind, American
postwar films basically remained white-bread
until a stoned Jack Nicholson, Peter Fonda, Dennis Hopper
and crew brought the biggie Hollywood studios
to their knees with the cheapo, culture-crashing *Easy Rider*.
I focused on an essay about the new movies
and superimposed a marquee touting that low-budget
runaway hit over the majestic doors of
St. Patrick's Cathedral and headlined it *Faith of Our Children*.
To American kids, *Easy Rider* had become
a cult film. Cardinal Terence Cooke and the Archdiocese of New York
were not pleased. To this day, whenever I stroll
past St. Paddy's, I always have a craving for popcorn.

AUGUST 1970
PRICE $1
Esquire
THE MAGAZINE FOR MEN
The New Movies:
Faith of Our
Children
See page 59
NEWSWEEK
PETER FONDA
DENNIS HOPPER
JACK NICHOLSON
IN EASY RIDER

THE KILLER COVER

In November 1970, while William Calley was awaiting trial for his role in the 1968 massacre of as many as 500 civilians at My Lai, *Esquire* scheduled an excerpt from *The Confessions of Lieutenant Calley*. With hardly a confession in sight, it was a book based on interviews by John Sack, who didn't believe in Calley's "innocence" as much as he believed in the guilt of President Nixon, General Westmoreland, and Secretary of Defense McNamara. "Tough subject for a cover. He's innocent until the army decides. And besides, he's a fall guy, a scapegoat for an atrocious war. Think about it," said editor Harold Hayes. "Can we get Calley to New York for a sitting?" I asked. "Sack probably can," he said, "but it depends on what you have in mind." I explained the shot: "We'll show him with a bunch of Vietnamese kids. Those who think he's innocent will say that proves it. Those who think he's guilty will say that proves it." Sack came to Carl Fischer's studio with the infamous lieutenant. Calley was edgy, almost suspicious. The presence of this young nobody who had suddenly caught the attention of the world and put a magnifying glass on the war gave that place an eerie feeling. I took "Rusty" aside to calm him down. I said that I myself was a Korean War veteran and told him some war stories so that he would "trust me." I explained the shoot: "Lieutenant, this picture will show that you're not afraid as far as your guilt is concerned. The picture will say, 'Here I am with these kids you're accusing me of killing. Whether you believe I'm guilty or innocent, at least read about my background and motivations.'" Calley posed solemnly but then grinned on cue, his blue eyes crinkling with cheer, surrounded by somber Vietnamese children (a deadly reminder of the kids he, and our leaders in the White House, had indeed murdered). But I knew full well that my cover could seem ambiguous. When I sent the finished cover to Hayes, he called to let me know that his office staff and *Esquire*'s masthead bureaucrats were plenty shook up. "Some detest it and some love it," he said. "You going to chicken out?" I asked. "Nope," he said. "We'll lose advertisers and we'll lose subscribers, but I have no choice. I'll never sleep again if I don't muster the courage to run it." The furor that arose over the Calley cover set the hawks and the doves at each other's throats all over America. (We now know that in the early months of 1969, the Ninth Infantry Division's Mekong Delta offensive claimed a "kill count" of 10,899, most of whom were innocent, unarmed Vietnamese civilians. It had been a war, shamefully, of many My Lais.)

Addendum: In 1971, a court martial convicted Calley of murder for killing 22 civilians (even though 500 men, women, and children had been massacred). Though sentenced to life in prison, he ended up serving a mere three years under house arrest after President Nixon reduced his sentence. In 2009, stirring the ghosts of a horrific episode, a contrite 66-year-old Calley finally "confessed" to a stunned Kiwanis Club of Greater Columbus audience when he softly spoke into a microphone: "There is not a day that goes by that I do not feel remorse for what happened that day in My Lai. I feel remorse for the Vietnamese who were killed, for their families, for the American soldiers involved, and their families. I am very sorry." A club member who witnessed the apology reported, "You could've heard a pin drop."

NOVEMBER 1970
PRICE $1

Esquire

THE MAGAZINE FOR MEN

The Confessions of Lt. Calley

See page 113

JACKIE OH!

Two vivid images are frozen in our collective memories:
The widow of our murdered president, draped over her husband's body in the fatal motorcade. Then, standing rigid in a blood-splattered dress beside Lyndon Johnson as he is sworn in. Her elegance under fire transformed a repulsive time of gore and national shame, somehow elevating it to a gaunt beauty. Then, Saint Jackie, the most public and revered woman in America, did the unimaginable: While still held heroic in her grief, this strangely spacey widow of the glorious JFK leaped into the oily embrace of the antihero Aristotle Onassis. As she abandoned the walls of the Kennedy compound for the blue waters of the Aegean, she boggled the minds of even the most loyal Jackie-lovers among us. Since, as far as we knew, Ari possessed no particular grace or attribute, we were forced to conclude that Mrs. Kennedy opted for the big bucks. We felt betrayed, our adoration besmirched. This special *Esquire* issue on *The Pursuit of Happiness* displayed our dismay. I rather vulgarly suggested that our Iconic Woman might want to see her new husband and protector as a youthful Mr. Olympia. Surprisingly, a business associate very close to Onassis told me that Aristotle laughed heartily when shown the cover. Go figure.

DECEMBER 1970
PRICE $1.50

Esquire

THE MAGAZINE FOR MEN

PORTRAIT OF A LOVING PARENT

Before Gay Talese's *Honor Thy Father* was published, *Esquire* ran a lengthy excerpt from the book on the Joseph Bonanno crime family. The book was a labor of love that had taken six years to write, after Talese had gained unprecedented access to Bonanno's inner circle. When I read the piece, I realized that its title was incredibly apt. Although *Honor Thy Father* was a major study of an Italian-American family enmeshed in the Mafia over two generations, it caught the deep love and loyalty between son and father, Salvatore "Bill" Bonanno, then in federal prison, and Joe, who died a ruined man. I felt the subject should be handled with a shocking reverence, rather than with Mafia-reporting sensationalism. So I got Talese to get me an entrée into the Bonanno home in New Jersey, where I hoped to get a family photo of the elder Bonanno. His widow was suspicious, but Gay explained in his lush Italian what we were after and why. Mamma Bonanno dug up a few '30s-style sepia shots, including this gem, and I knew I had the cover, one that expressed perfectly a son's respect for his father.
Many *Esquire* fans wondered how I could produce *en hommage* of a son who worshiped his *gangster* father—and a grease job on a daughter (Svetlana Stalin) who hated her *dictator* father. Maybe it's a basic character flaw on my part, but one of the axioms in the Bible that I've always lived by is "honor thy father," no matter what the old man's line of work.

P.S. I had no idea (nor did Harold Hayes) that this would be my last cover on the 10 x 12 5/8 inch canvas that I was privileged to create on—a sepia photograph of Bill Bonanno's old man in a great suit, hat, and coat, dignified, smooth, a throwback to an old-fashioned *Esquire* man, who happened also to be a mafioso. In retrospect, it was a stylish, beautiful cover out of the 1930s, when *Esquire* was born.

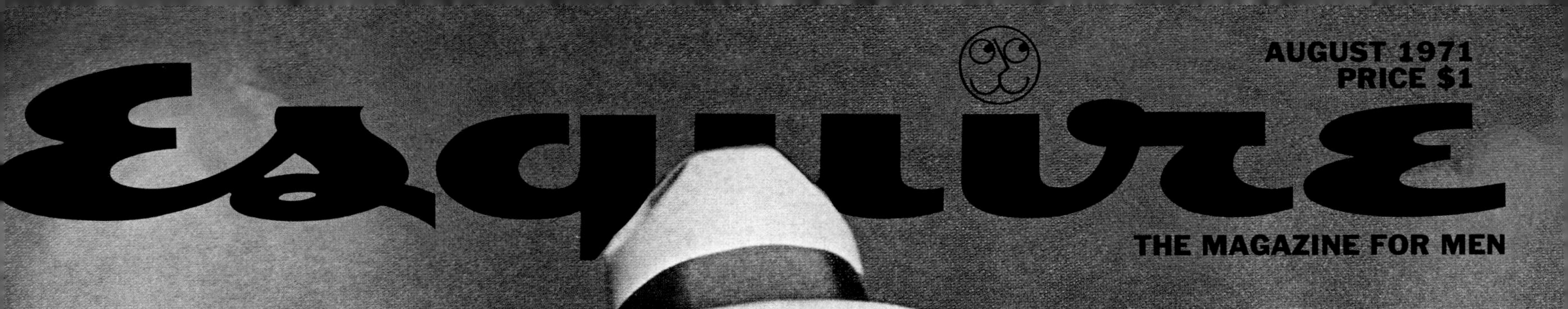

Honor thy Father

The story of Joe Bonanno and his son
by Gay Talese

THE INCREDIBLE SHRINKING MAGAZINE

A few weeks before this cover ran, Harold Hayes and I learned that the management of *Esquire* had, after 39 years, downsized the magazine—reducing it from *Life*-size to the smaller size that had become standard for magazines. With the help of my covers, Hayes had saved the magazine from bankruptcy in 1962, bringing fame and prosperity to *Esquire* for almost a decade. Now, with their nickel-and-dime downsizing of the magazine, the abominable No-men wrested power away from their great editor. When Hayes gave me the downsizing news, I bit the bullet. Smaller canvas it may have been, but the image on my first reduced-size cover leaped off the page and grabbed readers by the throat, becoming the biggest-selling newsstand cover in *Esquire* history. I showed the women's liberationist Germaine Greer looking ecstatic in the clutches of King Kong Norman Mailer—a parody of the running feud between them in public debates, on TV, and now on the pages of *Esquire*. When Norman Mailer saw this cover, he called Harold Hayes and challenged him to a brawl. Hayes chickened out and told the pugnacious penman to call the man responsible: me. We made a date to duke it out in Central Park. I showed up. Mailer didn't.

P.S. Editor Harold Hayes had always championed Mailer's talent, but the volatile writer was a constant irritant. In her book on *Esquire* in the 60's, *It Wasn't Pretty, Folks, But Didn't We Have Fun?*, author Carol Polsgrove tells the story of an installment of Mailer's *An American Dream*, a novel being written as it was published monthly in *Esquire*. The irascible Mailer put the word "shit" in at least 25 times—including some extras so he'd have room to negotiate with *Esquire*'s lawyers. After days of bickering, Hayes' final offer was,
"Norman, I'll trade two *shits* for a *fuck*."

SEPTEMBER 1971
PRICE $1

Esquire

THE MAGAZINE FOR MEN

Censored scenes from King Kong and...
Germaine Greer
on Norman Mailer!

GEORGE PETTY AND ME

"No more Esky dirty-old-man covers!"
(Esky, *Esquire*'s white-haired, pop-eyed playboy mascot,
had presided over each issue, symbolizing the intent
of its editors, until the Hayes-led revolution of the '60s.)
For nine years, I had been hard-nosed about
giving *Esquire* covers more than a periodic touch of their
old-time titillation. But when Harold Hayes conceived
an issue on America's "happy" 1940s, I rose to the occasion
and put a swinging George Petty pinup on
a swing-out cover. Just as the cool, unapproachable
Gibson Girl was the feminine ideal of young
men at the end of the 19th century, the swinging Petty Girl
became the ideal of their wide-eyed sons.
Starting in 1933, with the first issues of *Esquire* magazine,
George Petty's streamlined, long-legged,
airbrushed beauties took the country by storm, later going
on to greater heights as nose art on the fuselages
of countless World War II bombers. When I was a youngster,
Petty's lush American Dream Girls were right
up there with Botticelli's Venus, Rubens' flesh goddesses,
Manet's picnicking nude, Lachaise's she-women,
and the immortal Bettie Page, with more curves than even
God envisioned. Just putting my name
next to that of the great George Petty gave me a thrill.

Welcome back to the 40's

The last time America was happy. See Page 98

GEORGE LOIS

In 1970, for an ad promoting their magazine, Business Week *ran this Steve Horn portrait of Lois with the headline "What makes George Lois so humble?" Lois at first balked at posing as Jesus Christ, feeling that it could be construed as bad taste, but finally agreed (although he complained that he could have drowned in the 8-foot-deep tank of water).*

GEORGE LOIS WITH HIS SONS, LUKE AND HARRY JOE, AT AN EXHIBITION OF PAINTINGS BY HIS WIFE, ROSEMARY LEWANDOWSKI LOIS, 1967.

THE DAPPER HAROLD HAYES GETS THE LAST LAUGH AT A UNITED NATIONS ROAST OF GEORGE LOIS, 1972 (JIM CALLAWAY AT RIGHT).

A TRASHY ESQUIRE COVER

We are what we eat, and the proof of the pudding is in what we throw away. For the November 1971 issue, *Esquire*'s "investigative" reporters dug deep into the trash cans of some of the most interesting celebrities of our time to reveal their eating habits, reading material, Polaroid porn shots, drafts of love letters and gossip–all resulting in a somewhat trashy, in-depth study of their habits and lifestyles. My celebrity in the vegetative state was lifted from the Italian Mannerist paintings of Giuseppe Arcimboldo, which were greatly admired by Salvador Dali and other Surrealist painters. Arcimboldo's bizarre portrait heads of famous personalities of the 16th century were composed of vegetables, fruits, and tree roots. Greatly admired in their day, the art critics of today debate whether the "double" portraits were whimsical–or the product of a deranged mind.

THE MAGAZINE FOR MEN

You are what you throw away...

Secret garbage reports on:
Bob Dylan
Muhammad Ali
Abbie Hoffman
Neil Simon
See page 113

A COOL DUDE SUPERSTAR MODELING CLOTHES

Even through a decade of continuing prosperity under Harold Hayes' guidance, there were murmurs of discontent from the ad-sales gang. Could there be more "brownnose" service features and an end to those controversial covers? Couldn't the editors take fashion more seriously? So we decided to give the malcontents a photo story: *The 10 Best-Dressed Jocks*. The clotheshorse Walt "Clyde" Frazier of the New York Knicks was the world's coolest athlete; the only question was how to shoot a dude jock so that he looked like a superstar rather than a superstiff, the way male models usually looked. This way: Clyde, the quintessential smoothie, soars over the court, ball in hand, while guarded by that hurly-burly Irishman, Kevin Loughery. In the days before Photoshop, easier said than done. To heroically fly through the air without a rumple required a harness and wires–ordinarily not a big deal. However, a few hours after this shoot, Frazier would be on a plane with his teammates headed west to play the Los Angeles Lakers in the 1972 NBA Finals. Without Frazier, the Knicks' chances would nose-dive. If the harness slipped or if a wire snapped and something happened to Clyde (a torn muscle, a stubbed toe, a bruised pinkie), Knicks fans would never understand that art comes before championships. I held my breath. We shot the best-dressed jock. We lowered him lovingly. Then I exhaled.

P.S. A few nights later in L.A., Frazier heroically scored 27 points, with ten assists and seven rebounds, but the Knicks, alas, flew home losers.

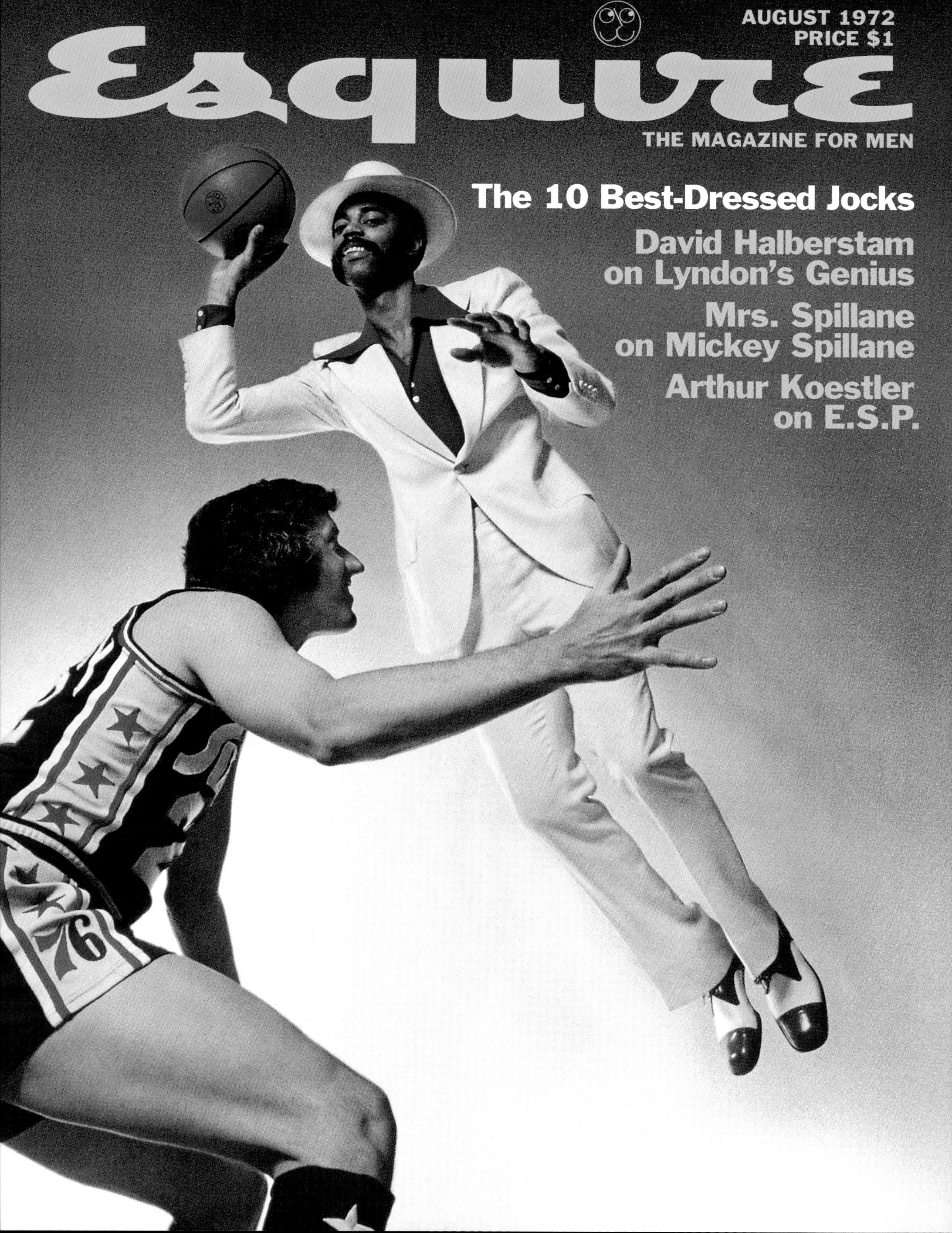
AUGUST 1972
PRICE $1
Esquire
THE MAGAZINE FOR MEN
The 10 Best-Dressed Jocks
David Halberstam
on Lyndon's Genius
Mrs. Spillane
on Mickey Spillane
Arthur Koestler
on E.S.P.
76

JACK NICHOLSON (AND, ULTIMATELY, ESQUIRE) TAKE A DIVE

The lead story in the October 1972 issue was all about the high jinks of L.A.'s Hollywood community. So photographer Timothy Galfas and I convinced the biggest movie star of them all to be photographed–bareass! Since the story related how hotdogging Jack Nicholson had greeted the writer wearing nothing but sandals and a hat, and chomping on a cigar, convincing the irascible rogue to pose in the buff was a cinch. He loved my covers and wanted to support what he called "the best magazine ever." *Esquire*'s ad boys, of course, once again thought "Lois has gone too far." But this time, even as the covers were roaring off the high-speed printers, management shouted, "Stop the presses!" Nicholson hadn't told his agent he had agreed to pose, and the concerned agent was threatening to sue the magazine. In 1972, nudity was no joke. Well, when Harold Hayes called to say the owners had killed the cover, in effect kowtowing to the power of the celebrities and their business agents, I knew it signaled the end of an illustrious road for Hayes at *Esquire*. Due entirely to Harold, *Esquire* was rolling in profits. While enriching its management, Hayes had single-handedly made the '60s *the* golden age of American journalism. But now, with contemptuous hubris, the illiterate money boys decided that *anyone* could edit *Esquire*. So they plotted to kill two villains at once: By kicking Hayes upstairs to be publisher, they would rid themselves of his editorial perfectionism *and* the tsuris of my covers. Always his own man, Harold Hayes elegantly told *Esquire*'s board of directors to kiss-off, then went on to help create and become the editorial producer of *20/20* for ABC-TV, serve as the chief troubleshooter for CBS Publications, create a matchless Ali-Frazier III fight program (with me), and write three terrific books inspired by his passion for Africa. Hayes died of a brain tumor on April 5,1989, at the age of 62, eternally undaunted, 16 years to the day after he had left *Esquire*.

P.S. Within a year of Harold's leaving *Esquire*, and with the mysterious absence of my "controversial" covers, the once-great magazine's circulation and advertising took an Olympic dive off the high board, arguably the most precipitous loss of readership in magazine history. W.R. Simmons, the media-research company that published total audience figures for magazines (including pass-along readers), reported that *Esquire*'s total audience had shrunk from seven million to four million readers, with a corresponding loss of half of its ad linage, with fears the magazine was going under. The journalism god had smote the philistines, but the glory days of *Esquire* came to a resounding end.

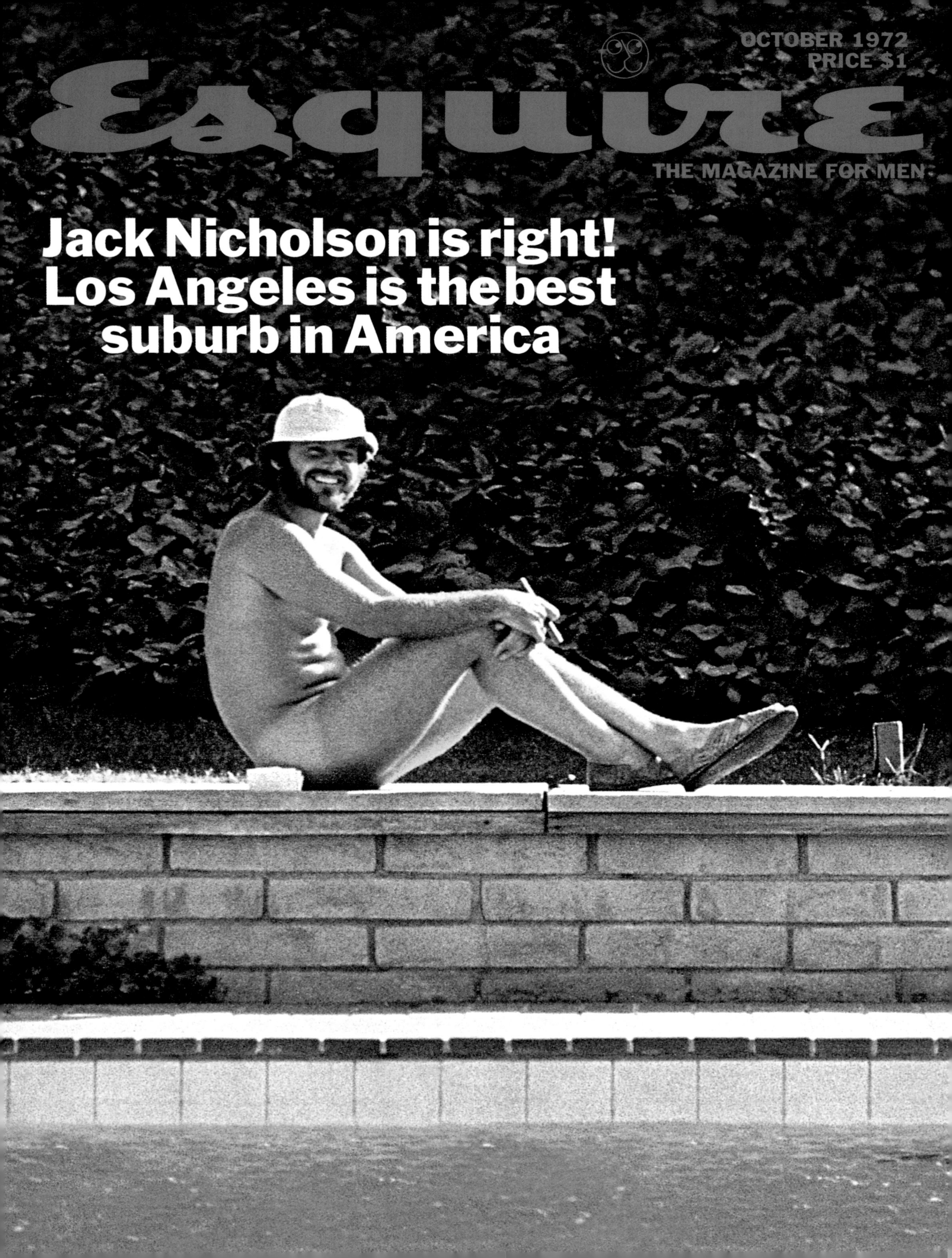
OCTOBER 1972
PRICE $1
Esquire
THE MAGAZINE FOR MEN
Jack Nicholson is right!
Los Angeles is the best
suburb in America

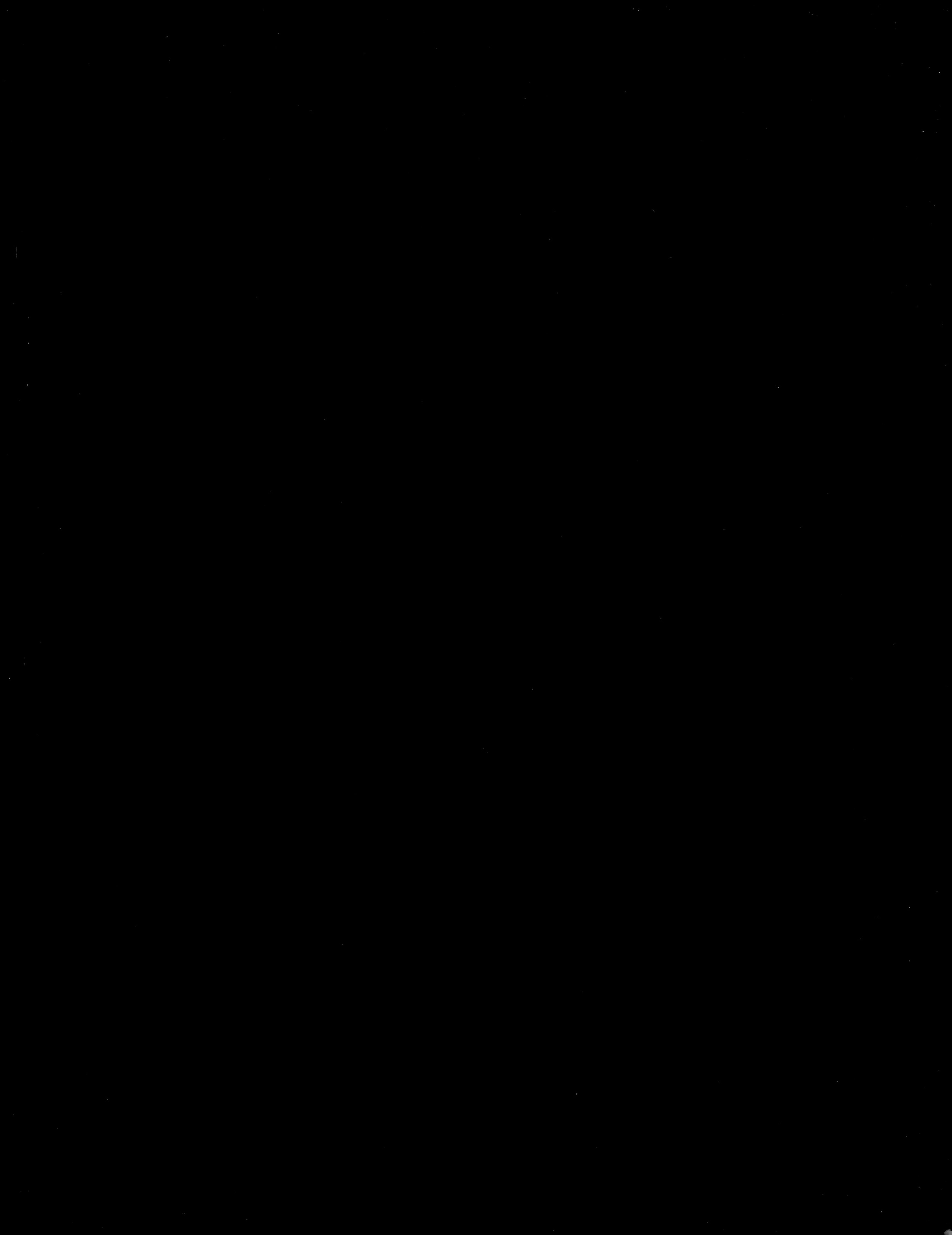

MEANWHILE, BACK AT THE AGENCY...

Until *New York*, no "city" magazine existed. Originally created as a concept and prototype design by George Lois in 1964 for a *New York Herald Tribune* magazine supplement, it then evolved into a weekly that has flourished for over 40 years.

"I want my MTV"

Oh, yes, MTV was a flop. Then Lois got Mick Jagger to get rock fans to call and yell, *I want my MTV!* Cable companies said, "OK!" And, as *Time* magazine reported, MTV instantly became "the most spectacular pop-culture phenomenon" of our time.

...PRODUCTS TRANSFORMED INTO POWER BRANDS, EACH BASED ON A BIG IDEA.

In 1982, it was a newspaper everybody loved —except advertisers! Lois woke them up by showing how *USA Today*, with jumped-up graphics and brisk reporting, nailed the TV generation. Another power brand hot off the presses.

A lot of media people are saying USA TODAY is neither fish nor fowl.

They're right!

THE ADVERTISING MIGHT OF USA TODAY

To our readers, we're a newspaper–bold, exciting, colorful and unique. To many of our advertisers, we're a newsmagazine–bold, exciting, colorful and unique. The truth is, we don't much care what you call us. Just as long as you call us.

Call Valerie Salembier at (212) 715-5380

Slomin's Home Security System was a sleepy Long Island company. Lois changed their name to *The Slomin's Shield* with a memorable TV campaign, and he introduced Alarmo, an animated logo who muscled Slomin's into the power brand of home security.

THE SLOMIN'S SHIELD™
HOME SECURITY SYSTEM

In 1985, Tommy Hilfiger was an unknown until Lois ran this one outrageous ad—and overnight, a star was worn!

THE 4 GREAT AMERICAN DESIGNERS FOR MEN ARE:

R_____ L_____
P____ E____
C_____ K____
T____ H_______

THIS IS THE LOGO OF THE LEAST KNOWN OF THE FOUR

In most households, the first three names are household words. Get ready to add another. His first name (hint) is Tommy. The second name is not so easy. But in a few short months everybody in America will know there's a new look in town and a new name at the top. Tommy's clothes are easy-going without being too casual, classic without being predictable. He calls them classics with a twist. The other three designers call them competition.

282 Columbus Avenue
at 73rd Street
New York, New York 10023
(212) 877-1270

© 1985 MURJANI

In 1982, there were just six lonely locations with a big marketing idea: Lubricating your car in minutes! But nobody cared until Lois' new logo and ad campaign grew Jiffy Lube into the more than 2,000-unit power brand that changed the way America changed its oil.

In 1994, almost overnight, Lois changed the perception of ESPN as a denigrated "demolition derby" sports channel when he shoved ESPN in America's face with his *In Your Face* TV campaign—transforming them from a "mickey-mouse" network to the power network of sports!

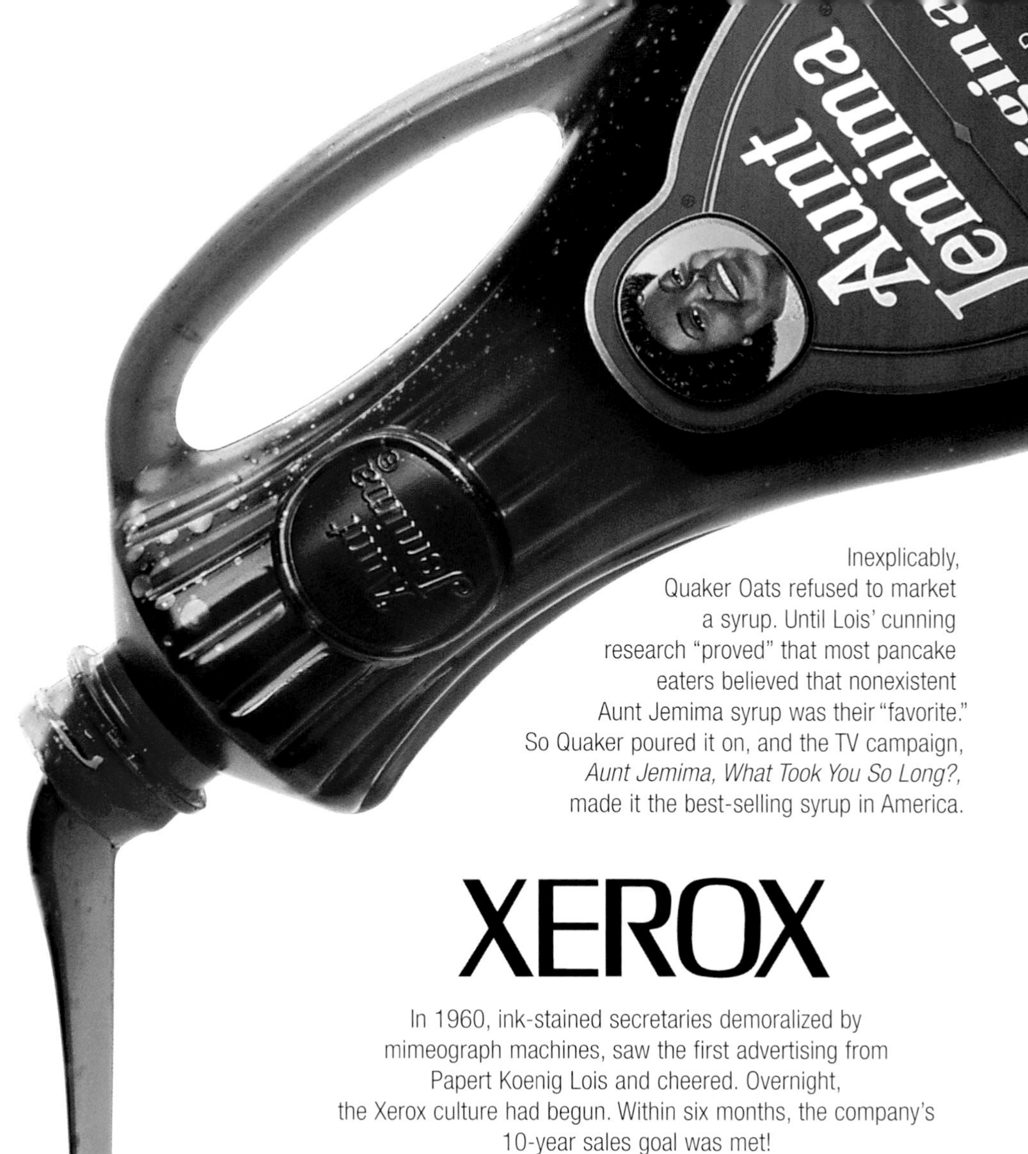

Inexplicably, Quaker Oats refused to market a syrup. Until Lois' cunning research "proved" that most pancake eaters believed that nonexistent Aunt Jemima syrup was their "favorite." So Quaker poured it on, and the TV campaign, *Aunt Jemima, What Took You So Long?,* made it the best-selling syrup in America.

XEROX

In 1960, ink-stained secretaries demoralized by mimeograph machines, saw the first advertising from Papert Koenig Lois and cheered. Overnight, the Xerox culture had begun. Within six months, the company's 10-year sales goal was met!

THE FOUR SEASONS

In 1974, The Four Seasons restaurant had dwindled into a lackluster tourist trap. So Lois promised attention from its two new owners with his *The Two of Us* ad campaign and transformed its Grill Room by inventing the *Power Lunch* and creating the nutritious *Spa Cuisine*. Today, even *he* has trouble getting a reservation there.

Less than a year after President Kennedy was assassinated, Robert, characterized by detractors as his "ruthless little brother" and stuck with the stigma of being a "carpetbagger," ran for the U.S. Senate. Lois' campaign, *Let's Put Robert Kennedy to Work For New York*, was a fast counterattack, and Bobby was on his way to greatness when he met the same fate as his big brother.

In 1980, Stouffer's snickered at Lois' idea of a frozen gourmet fitness food line. Then the company saw his name for it, *Lean Cuisine*, and a new and dynamic marketing category hit the marketplace.

PAPERT KOENIG LOIS ADVERTISING

Founded in 1960 by Fred Papert, Julian Koenig, and George Lois.

LOIS HOLLAND CALLAWAY ADVERTISING

Founded in 1967 by George Lois, Ron Holland, and Jim Callaway.

LOIS PITTS GERSHON ADVERTISING

Founded in 1978 by George Lois, Bill Pitts, and Dick Gershon.

LOIS/USA ADVERTISING

(Upon the retirement of Pitts and Gershon, in 1995.)

RON HOLLAND (STANDING), GEORGE LOIS,
JIM CALLAWAY, AND BILL PITTS PRESENTING
TO OLIVETTI CLIENT GIL WINTERING
IN THE EARLY '70s.

The day George Lois stopped creating *Esquire* covers, in his spare moments away from his ad agency, he started his first book, *George, be careful*, which led to a collection of books that continue to teach and inspire the design and media communities throughout the world.

George, be careful
(Saturday Review Press, 1972), an autobiography.

The Art of Advertising (Abrams, 1976), praised as "the bible of mass communications."

$ellebrity
(Phaidon, 2003), explores how Lois' ad campaigns use celebrities in fresh and outrageous ways.

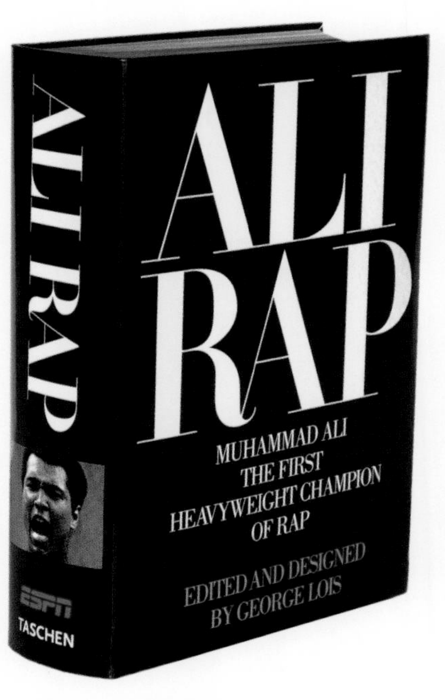

Ali Rap, The First Heavyweight Champion of Rap
(Taschen/ESPN, 2006), a compilation of more than 300 rap rhythms, witticisms, insults, and wisecracks from Muhammad Ali.

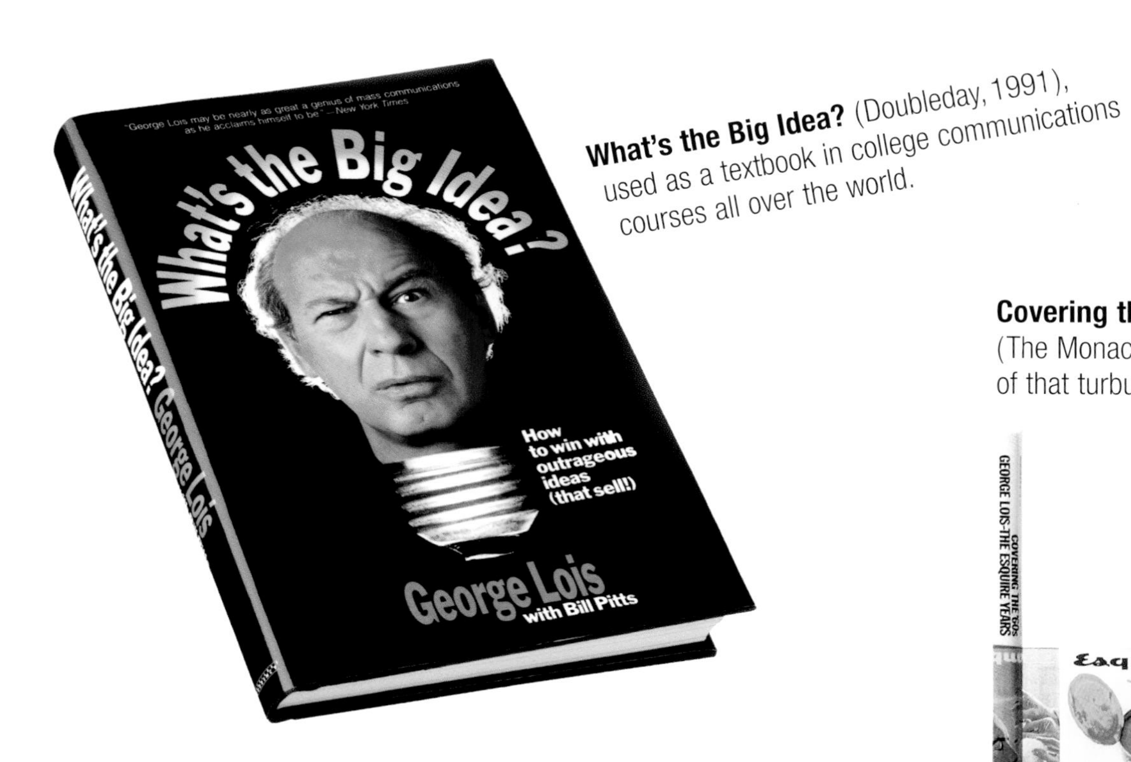

What's the Big Idea? (Doubleday, 1991), used as a textbook in college communications courses all over the world.

Covering the '60s
(The Monacelli Press, 1996), presents Lois' *Esquire* covers of that turbulent decade.

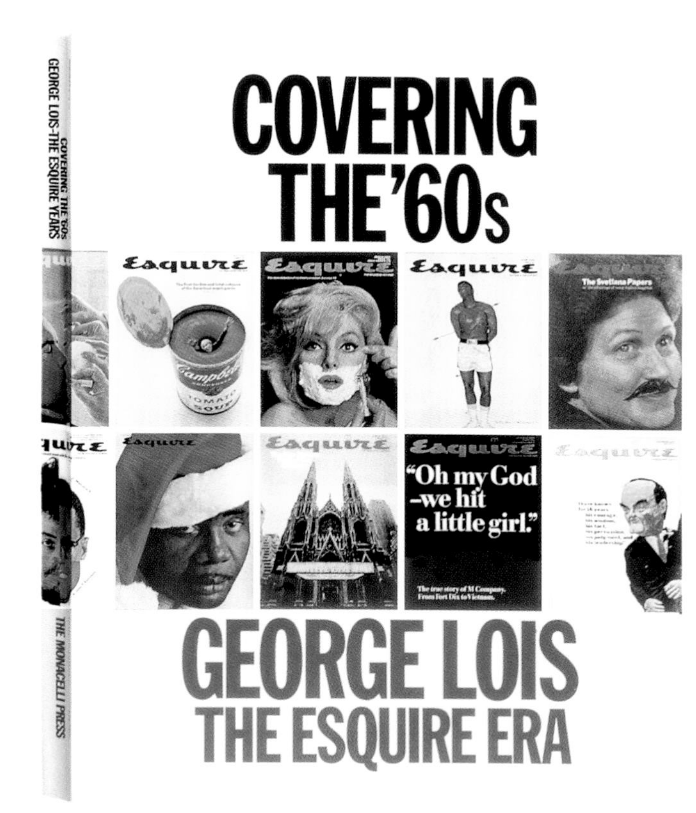

Iconic America (Rizzoli/Universe, 2007), a roller-coaster ride through the eye-popping panorama of American pop culture.

George Lois on His Creation of The Big Idea
(Assouline, 2008), a mind-boggling archeological dig revealing the influences on 100 of his Big Ideas.

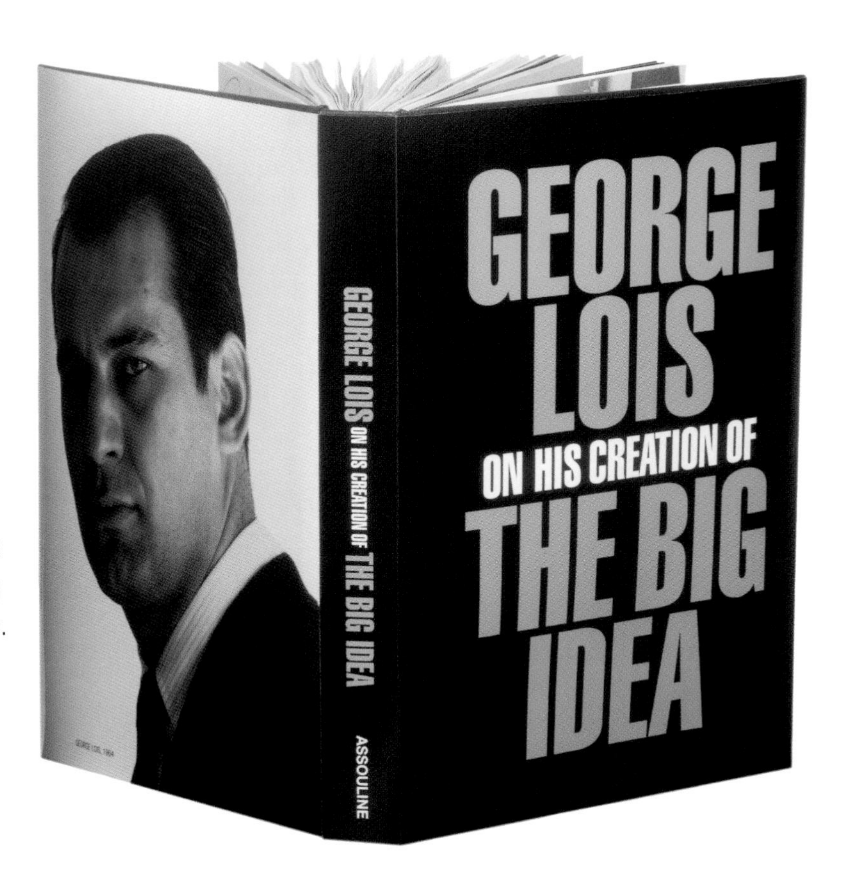

WHY ARE THESE MEN LAUGHING?

In an anthology of the chronicle of the '60s, *Esquire* editor Harold Hayes characterized the efforts of his New Journalism writers (Norman Mailer, William Styron, Gay Talese, Tom Wolfe, Gore Vidal, John Sack, James Baldwin, Garry Wills, Richard Rovere, Peter Bogdanovich, and 40 others), along with my visual record of the most turbulent decade in American history, as a monthly visceral experience that resolutely "smiled through the apocalypse."

SMILING THROUGH THE APOCALYPSE:
ESQUIRE'S HISTORY OF THE SIXTIES
EDITED BY HAROLD HAYES
(THE McCALL PUBLISHING CO., 1970)

HAROLD HAYES
AND GEORGE LOIS IN 1982,
20 YEARS AFTER THEIR
FIRST COLLABORATION, REMINISCING
ABOUT THEIR ESQUIRE *GLORY DAYS,*
NOW KNOWN AS THE GOLDEN AGE OF
JOURNALISM IN AMERICA.

THE MAGAZINE FOR MEN

Esquire
DECEMBER 1962
PRICE $1.50
THE MAGAZINE FOR MEN
"Merry Christmas. I'm the 100th G.I. killed in Vietnam."

Esquire
AUGUST 1963
PRICE 60c
THE MAGAZINE FOR MEN
THE CLEOPATRA PAPERS. ABSOLUTELY, POSITIVELY, THE LAST WORD. NO KIDDING. P. 33

Esquire
OCTOBER, 1963
PRICE 60c
THE MAGAZINE FOR MEN
INSIDE THE SQUARE: GLAMOR. OUTSIDE: REAL LIFE. TO LEARN THE DIFFERENCE, SEE PAGE 125

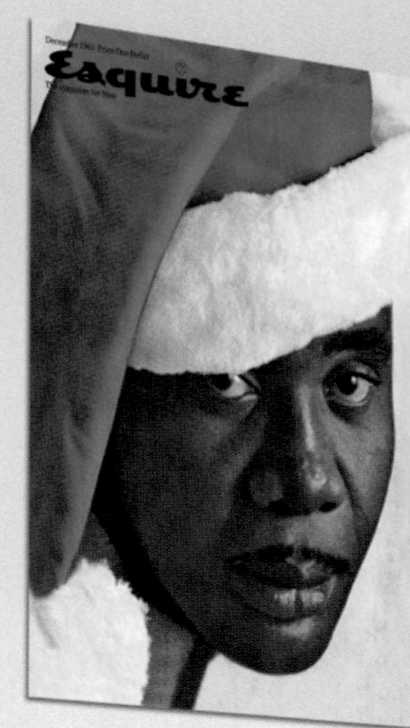

Esquire

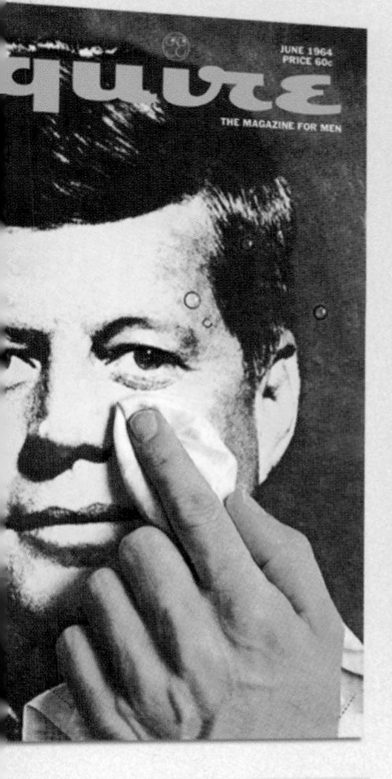

JUNE 1964
PRICE 60c
THE MAGAZINE FOR MEN

Esquire
MARCH 1965
PRICE 75c
The masculinization of the American woman. See page 76
THE MAGAZINE FOR MEN

Esquire
OCTOBER 1965
PRICE 75c
THE MAGAZINE FOR MEN
Heaven help him - he's going to play 60 minutes of pro ball
62

Esquire
JULY 1966
PRICE 75c
THE MAGAZINE FOR MEN
What's DiMaggio doing with himself these days?

Esquire
THE MAGAZINE FOR MEN
How our red blooded campus heroes are beating the draft:

SEPTEMBER 1967
PRICE $1
COLLEGE ISSUE
r in Vietnam is hell, you ought to see
on campus, baby.

Esquire
THE MAGAZINE FOR MEN
JULY 1965
PRICE 75c
Does today's teen-ager influence the adult world? "Ridiculous." says Ed Sullivan.

Esquire
AUGUST 1966
PRICE 75c
THE MAGAZINE FOR MEN
In Defense of Cassius Clay
By Floyd Patterson

Esquire
MAY 1967
PRICE 75c
THE MAGAZINE FOR MEN
Why Jack Ruby killed Lee Oswald... an untold story.

Esquire
FEBRUARY 1967
PRICE 75c
THE MAGAZINE FOR MEN
The New American Woman: through at 21.

Jean Genet,
William Burroughs,
Terry Southern,
John Sack,
Chicago!

Esquire
FEBRUARY 1968
PRICE $1
THE MAGAZINE FOR MEN

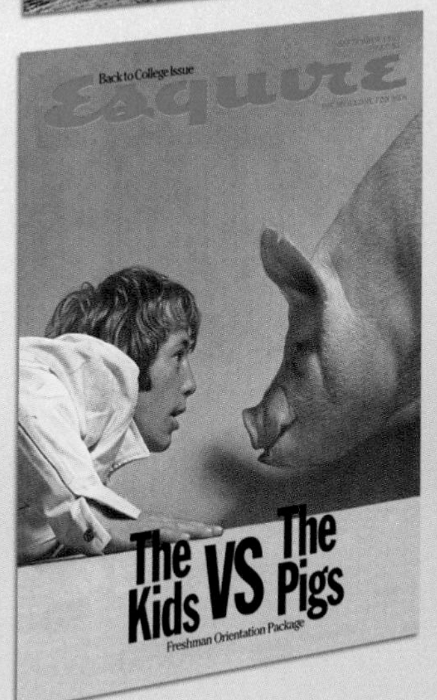

Back to College Issue
Esquire
The Kids VS The Pigs
Freshman Orientation Package

NOVEMBER 1970
PRICE $1
Esquire
THE MAGAZINE FOR MEN
The Confessions of Lt. Calley

GEORGE LOIS
THE ESQUIRE COVERS

From 1962 to 1972, George Lois changed the face of magazine design with his covers for Esquire, creating some of the most arresting and iconic images in the history of the magazine cover. With his uniquely uncompromising point of view, Lois exploited the communicative power of the mass-circulated front page to stimulate minds and provoke public debate. The sensational effect these covers had on the public was an obvious advantage for Esquire's circulation, but their lasting importance was that they forced Americans to confront controversial issues such as racism, feminism, religion, and the Vietnam War. These images hit the public like a punch in the face, their messages artfully communicated with force and immediacy.

When Harold Hayes became Esquire's editor in 1961, the monthly men's magazine founded in 1933 had passed its peak in the 1940s and was on the verge of bankruptcy. He needed to renew its image and recognized the cover as the most visible and important page for public recognition. He met with Lois, who suggested that a single designer produce the cover instead of the "design-by-consensus" approach Hayes had taken with his staff. Hayes asked Lois to design one cover for him. Lois daringly called the upcoming boxing match in favor of underdog Sonny Liston by showing the heavily favored Floyd Patterson knocked-out and alone in the arena. This October 1962 cover generated the largest newsstand sales in Esquire's history – and Lois continued designing covers for Harold Hayes as Esquire's circulation exploded in the decade that is now thought of as the Golden Age of Journalism.

The Museum of Modern Art installs George Lois's iconic Esquire covers and presents thirty-two of them that serve as a visual timeline of American culture in the 1960s and early 1970s, alongside original artwork, photographs, contact sheets, and other ephemera as a means of explaining the creative process behind these deceptively simple yet complex designs. With the wholehearted support of Esquire editor Harold Hayes and the collaboration of photographers Carl Fischer, Timothy Galfas, Art Kane, Harold Krieger, Ira Mazer, Dick Richards, and Tasso Vendikos, the full extent of Lois's design talent shines as he translated daring ideas into visually stunning, eloquent images. As paradigms of graphic and communication design, the covers are significant additions to MoMA's collection.

Viewed as a collection now, nearly fifty years since they first appeared on the newsstands, the covers serve as a visual time line and a window onto the turbulent events of the 1960s. Initially received as jarring and prescient statements, Lois' Esquire covers have since become essential to the iconography of American culture.

"MoMA celebrates Esquire*'s George Lois decade with a yearlong exhibition of his iconic covers, thereafter to be returned to the museum's permanent collection. The consummately rendered covers are not so much the product of a famous adman as the work of a brilliant graphic designer with a distinctive, visceral approach to art direction."*

VANITY FAIR

EPILOGUE

"WHY CAN'T THEY CREATE 'GEORGE LOIS COVERS' ANYMORE"

The oft-asked question repeated in editorial offices and by cultural afficionados throughout the world is partly answered by the great portrait photographer, **Annie Leibovitz**, in her book of memoirs, *Annie Leibovitz at Work* (Random House, 2008). In a chapter she entitles *Conceptual Pictures*, she bears witness to the fears that "idea" covers do not sell: "Creating a portrait with a strong concept was in past a response to taking so many cover pictures for *Rolling Stone*. I thought a cover picture should have an idea. I still do, although it's become more and more difficult to do conceptual covers. Covers have to sell magazines, and publishers are always trying to figure out what's effective and what isn't. The great master of the conceptual cover was the art director George Lois, who created so many legendary covers for *Esquire* in the '60s. When Muhammad Ali was convicted of draft evasion and stripped of his heavyweight boxing title, Lois had him photographed as the martyred Saint Sebastian, with arrows sticking out of his body. And he drowned Andy Warhol in a can of Campbell's soup." Leibovitz goes on to write, "In the early days at *Rolling Stone*, the subject of the cover was whatever Jann Wenner was interested in, or whatever some writer had finally finished. Now covers are always pegged to something. And who's on the cover makes a big difference. For a while, Jann thought that all *Rolling Stone* covers should be shot against a seamless white backdrop, in the style of Richard Avedon. There is a recurring idea that there should be some kind of formula for the cover—that all the covers should look the same and that familiarity sells. Not many chances are taken."

Obviously the fear of an ambitious cover with a powerful idea stems from the hierarchy of the magazine. **Frank DiGiacomo** referred to that paralyzing fear in a *Vanity Fair* article (January, 2007): "To a magazine industry that, like the rest of the culture, was still throwing off the dull, mannered structures of the '50s, Harold Hayes' arrangement with Lois was shocking. Admen sold soap, not magazines. But provocation, on many levels, was exactly what Hayes sought. Since taking the reins of *Esquire* two years earlier, he had pushed to make every column inch of the magazine sing with the brash authority that made news and upset the powers that be. In Lois, he had struck gold. Here was someone who could articulate that irreverence—in visual terms—on the most important page of the magazine, once a month. And then Hayes did what he did with his writers: He stepped back and let Lois do his thing." In the same article, **Nora Ephron** commented, "Hayes had the exact thing that all of the great editors and producers and studio heads and politicians have, which is, he absolutely trusted his gut."

Nick Paumgarten, of *The New Yorker*, tackled the question head-on in *The Talk of the Town* (April, 2008): "George Lois' *Esquire* covers from the '60s, widely celebrated and frequently (if faintheartedly) imitated, created a visual language that people in the media still feel they must learn to understand, if not speak well...magazine editors regularly call Lois to tell him that they have produced 'Lois covers' of their own—worthy homages, at least—and his response tends to be 'I don't think so.' In general, he disdains the wan, cluttered magazine covers of today. 'They go out and test: Do you like this person? Do you like the blurbs? Do you like this blurb better than this blurb? It's unbelievable. I'd do a cover that would knock your eyeballs out. Whether you liked it or hated it, you knew there was a magazine that was pumping blood. Now everyone's sweating bullets. They all sit there with their cover, their this and their that, their testing, who's the guy gonna be, who's the woman gonna be. Do we do tits and ass. They're all going wacko on their covers, and the covers get worse and worse.'"

And **James Wolcott** nails it in *Vanity Fair* (February, 2003): "In the advertising world, Lois can spot traces of his influence among 'a lot of guys that came after me that I inspired...' but when he visits a newsstand, however, he feels that his legacy were written in vanishing ink. Although the audacious covers he designed for *Esquire* in the '60s and early '70s are lauded as one of the marathon achievements in magazine history, these testimonials are nothing but talk—magazines have never played it safer. Circulation soared during the Hayes-Lois years and dove when they left, yet none seems to have picked up the baton, or the hint." As far as the possibility of a new graphic talent that could strike from out of the blue in the magazine world, Wolcott considers the possibility with this conclusion: "No editor worth his personal stationery wants to forgo prerogative and strike the dream deal that Lois enjoyed with Hayes, who committed himself to run whatever cover Lois finally dropped on his desk, damn the primal screams of outraged advertisers and cranky subscribers."

P.S. So here are my words of advice to those editors, editorial designers, and publishers who are handcuffed by their self-imposed insistence on sicko-phant, look-alike covers (each plastered with a torrent of story blurbs), who take comfort in the belief that "idea covers" cannot sell in today's media culture. Great magazine covers with big, edgy ideas that make powerful statements about America's politics and culture—through wit, irony, and even ambiguity—can force-feed an irresistable taste of a magazine's content, and issue after issue create a titanic stir in the American psyche. A magazine cover has a nanosecond to connect, to surprise, to excite, to *sell*. (When Harold Hayes was given the editorship of *Esquire* in the early 1960s, he intuitively felt the need to publish idea covers for his thinking man's magazine, but his collaborative process with his staff was an abysmal failure.) Now, more than ever, amid your cacophony of dull, mind-numbing covers of mindless celebrities, your magazine has the weekly or monthly opportunity to inspire the world with passionate images and words that spring from the human mind and heart. All that's needed is to find a young George Lois—and let him "do his thing."

DEDICATION

In 1968, the World Heavyweight Champion Muhammad Ali sardonically spoke of himself as "America's Public Enemy No. 1." To visually dramatize his principled, even prophetic stand against the Vietnam War, as he was excruciatingly waiting for the U.S. Supreme Court to decide his fate, Ali posed for my April 1968 *Esquire* cover as the martyr Saint Sebastian (see page 114). As I was directing the photo session, Muhammad called out to me, "George, George," pointed to each of the arrows "piercing his body," and indicated each of his tormentors: "Lyndon Johnson…Robert McNamara…General Westmoreland…Dean Rusk… Clark Clifford…Hubert Humphrey!" Thirty-five years later, for a *Vanity Fair* article about my book *$ellebrity*, I arranged a photo shoot of Ali and me, ol' pals in our war against the war. Afflicted with Parkinson's disease, the champ sat with me in the corner of a boxing ring at his Michigan compound, as war photographer David Turnley stood below us, clicking away. Turnley paused and whispered to me, "George, Ali is asleep—what should I do?" "Nahh—no way," I blurted out. "He's faking you out—shoot away." Ali turned to me, popped open one eye, and pointed behind him to a giant, life-size blowup of the Saint Sebastian cover, and then to imaginary arrows stuck in his now-debilitated body, and indicated, once again, his onetime tormentors, one-by-one, the same names, in the same exact order: "Lyndon Johnson…Robert McNamara…General Westmoreland…Dean Rusk… Clark Clifford…Hubert Humphrey."

With fond memories and devotion, I humbly dedicate this book to the iconic Muhammad Ali, a true superhero in the annals of American history and the worldwide ambassador of courage and conviction. Since the 1960s, Ali has had a home in our hearts, and now, depicted as a modern-day Saint Sebastian, he has a home at the Museum of Modern Art in New York City.

GEORGE LOIS

MUHAMMAD ALI AND GEORGE LOIS, NOV. 6, 2002

PHOTOGRAPHY CREDITS

4-5 Luke Lois **7** Timothy Galfas **6-7** Timothy Galfas Studio **8** Courtesy Tom Hayes, Harold Hayes Estate
9 Timothy Galfas **15** Matthew DeGennaro **16-20** Collection of George Lois **21** Courtesy Tom Hayes, Harold Hayes Estate
22 Timothy Galfas **23** Courtesy Tom Hayes, Harold Hayes Estate **26-27** Timothy Galfas **29** Carl Fischer
33 book: Luke Lois / Harry Lois in florist shop: Collection of George Lois **35** Courtesy Tom Hayes, Harold Hayes Estate
39 Oct 62: Harold Krieger **41** Dec 62: Collection of George Lois **43** Feb 63: Timothy Galfas
45 Mar 63: Stock **47** May 63: Timothy Galfas **49** Jun 63: Carl Fischer **51** Aug 63: Carl Fischer
52-53 Collection of George Lois **55** Oct 63: Art Kane **57** Dec 63: Carl Fischer **59** Feb 63: Timothy Galfas
61 Mar 64: Carl Fischer **63** Apr 64: Carl Fischer / modelmaker: Stan Glaubach **65** Jun 64: Carl Fischer
67 Nov 64: Timothy Galfas **69** Timothy Galfas Studio **71** Mar 65: Carl Fischer **73** May 65: Harold Krieger
75 July 65: Carl Fischer **77** Sep 65: photos: Stock **79** Oct 65: Carl Fischer **81** Nov 65: Carl Fischer / face of LBJ: Stock
83 Apr 66: art by Edward Sorel **85** Jun 66: Carl Fischer **87** July 66: Carl Fischer **89** Aug 66: Carl Fischer
91 Sep 66: Carl Fischer **95** Nov 66: Carl Fischer / face of LBJ: Stock / dummy: Stan Glaubach
97 Bob Kiger, from the Collection of Dean Dexter **99** Dec 66: Timothy Galfas **101** Feb 67: Carl Fischer
103 May 67: Dick Richards **105** July 67: Timothy Galfas **107** Sep 67: Carl Fischer
109 Nov 67: Stock / mustache: George Lois **111** Dec 67: Carl Fischer **113** Feb 68: Carl Fischer **115** Apr 68: Carl Fischer
116-117 Carl Fischer Studio **119** May 68: Nixon: Stock / hands: Carl Fischer **121** July 68: Carl Fischer
123 Aug 68: Dick Richards **125** Sep 68: Carl Fischer **127** Oct 68: Arlington and figures: Carl Fischer / faces: Stock
129 Nov 68: Carl Fischer **131** Dec. 68: Carl Fischer **133** Mar 69: Tasso Vendikos **134-135** Carl Fischer
137 May 69: Carl Fischer **199** July 69: Stock **141** Aug 69: Carl Fischer **143** Sep 69: Carl Fischer **145** Nov 69: Ira Mazer
146-147 Collection of George Lois **148-149** George Kalinsky **151** July 70: Carl Fischer
153 Aug 70: Carl Fischer **155** Nov 70: Carl Fischer **157** Dec 70: Timothy Galfas / face: Stock
159 Aug 71: Collection of the Bonanno family **161** Sep 71: Carl Fischer / faces: Stock **163** Oct 71: art by George Petty
165 Steve Horn **166** Rosemary Lois **167** Tasso Vendikos **169** Nov 71: art by Arcimboldo
171 Aug 72: Carl Fischer **173** Oct 72 Timothy Galfas **178-181** Collection of George Lois **182-183** books: Luke Lois
184-185 Michael Soluri **187** Tom Courtos **188** David Turnley

INDEX